THE NEGLECTED ETHIC

The McGRAW-HILL Nursing Studies Series

Chapple and Drew: Fundamentals of Nursing
Bickerton, Sampson, and Boylan: Nursing: Theory and Practice
Burrowes and Reakes: First Level General Nursing
Hoy and Robbins: The Profession of Nursing
Hoy: Nature and Causation of Disease

The Neglected Ethic
Cultural and Religious Factors in the Care of Patients

A C M Sampson, SRN, RNT

McGRAW-HILL Book Company (UK) Limited

London · New York · St Louis · San Francisco · Auckland · Bogotá
Guatemala · Hamburg · Johannesburg · Lisbon · Madrid · Mexico
Montreal · New Delhi · Panama · Paris · San Juan · São Paulo
Singapore · Sydney · Tokyo · Toronto

Published by
McGRAW-HILL Book Company (UK) Limited
MAIDENHEAD · BERKSHIRE · ENGLAND

British Library Cataloguing in Publication Data

Sampson, A. C. M.,
    The neglected ethic: cultural and religious
    factors in the care of patients.—(McGraw-Hill
    nursing studies series)
    1. Medical personnel and patient
    2. Medicine and religion
    I. Title
    610.69'6   RT86.5

    ISBN 0-07-084645-6

Library of Congress Cataloging in Publication Data

Sampson, A. C. M.
    The neglected ethic.
    (McGraw-Hill nursing studies series)
    Bibliography: p.
    Includes index.
    1. Social medicine. 2. Medicine and religion.
    3. Medical anthropology. 4. Medical ethics.
    5. Minorities—Medical care—Great Britain.
    I. Title. II. Series.
    RA418.S265   291.1/78321   81-13711
    ISBN 0-07-084645-6   SAM   AACR2

12345 MAC 8432

Typeset in Baskerville by Styleset Limited · Salisbury · Wiltshire and
printed and bound in Great Britain by Mackays of Chatham Ltd

CONTENTS

Preface   vii

Acknowledgements   xi

Author's note   xiii

1. Introduction and theoretical background   1
2. A general approach to religious and cultural factors   8
3. Some cultural aspects of care of patients   15
4. Religions and religious factors   47
5. The teaching of medical and nursing ethics   102

Selected bibliography   108

Index   110

PREFACE

This book provides a brief account of the religions and cultures of patients who are most likely to be nursed in British hospitals. Its aim is to give nurses, doctors, midwives, health visitors and others including therapists, psychologists, dieticians, social workers and ministers of religion working with the sick and their families, an insight into the possible implications of a patient's religion and culture as these may affect the form of care required, or even the medical treatment acceptable to the patient and his family. It is not enough, however, to absorb detailed information on the culture and religions of different ethnic groups and on the attitudes towards care and treatment which arise from them, some general perspective is also needed on the overall ethical problems facing the medical and nursing professions. Since the essence of an ethical judgement or decision often derives from its context or is strongly coloured by it, and must always be seen – if only subconsciously – against its general theoretical background, the introduction which follows is designed to provide (for students especially) something of this background.

Part 2 gives an overall view of the various worldwide religions and the cultural factors that arise from them. While Parts 3 and 4 are arranged in the form of alphabetical indexes and cover in detail the cultural aspects of the care of patients, and religion and religious factors.

The teaching of medical and nursing ethics is addressed in Part 5, where an attempt is made to examine the relative merits and integration of the theoretical and practical aspects of training and which develops arguments for a multidisciplinary approach.

This book does not aspire to being a treatise on world religions and cultures, nor an analysis of the moral dilemmas in medicine, nor a compendium of nursing ethics, nor a philosophical dissertation – although it cannot avoid touching upon all these areas. It is, essentially, an introduction which is designed to encourage practitioners and students alike to become more aware of their patients' backgrounds and to be more sensitive to their needs.

Religion and culture form part of the dynamism of life, wherein theory and practice can be notoriously divergent. In practice, very few individuals respond as a total stereotype of their cultural or religious group. Cultural background or religion may be more or less important to the individual and, where they are important, a person's interpretations may be far from orthodox. Herein lies one difficulty in compiling a useful textbook of this kind. To compound this problem, more extensive travel, working abroad, international radio and television, the

commonplace worldwide circulation of translated literature, the mingling of cultures on the mass scale of package holidays abroad, immigration and increasing intermarriage, have both diluted and mingled the
'pure' ethnic and religious archetypes which, for the sake of clarity,
conciseness and practicality have been set out in this book.

Every patient, of course, presents varied problems in his medical,
mental and spiritual needs. Textbooks abound on the ingredients of
medical and mental care, which must be prescribed in the right propor-
tions for each individual case. This book is an attempt to provide the
basic ingredients of understanding in the fields of culture and religion,
which require no less discrimination in their practical application. It is
a starting point for reflection, further study and for training, practice
and experience.

In putting it together, I have tried to strike a balance between making
it readable as a whole, and useful as a work for quick reference on a
busy hospital ward. The two, of course, are incompatible, and I have
leaned towards the latter, more practical form; hence the subheadings
and tabulations and, inevitably, some repetition in order to make any
section referred to reasonably complete in itself. Sometimes the reader
is referred to other pages in order to complete the reference required.
But, at the cost of some repetition, this tiresome habit has been kept to
a minimum.

In attempting to produce a compact and handy volume I have
confined my 'ingredients' to the main religious and cultural groups
likely to be found in British hospitals. By virtue of our imperial past
and worldwide connections, even today, this does in fact cover as wide
a spectrum as may be found in any other country; so this book may be
of value in many countries of the world. However, no attempt has been
made to include *all* religious sects and cultures, and any such omissions
do not necessarily reflect upon the numerical or other importance of a
particular group. Some may be omitted because they do not differ
materially from the more predominant sections of a group, or because
they are unlikely to have a serious impact on the normal medical and
nursing procedures in British hospitals today. For others that may have
been omitted I apologize for my ignorance.

When research began on this subject, I was dismayed to find how
little has been written about it. Most of the material available covered
either one aspect of the whole or was a sectional viewpoint of one
religious or cultural group. The lack of attention to these aspects of
patient care has always been excused as being due to pressure on training programmes. But the apparent lack of official concern which is
reflected in this dearth of research came as an unexpected shock. Hence
'the neglected ethic' of the title. There are thousands of devoted doctors, nurses, ministers and social workers of all kinds who have been
grappling with the problems presented in this book for much longer

than I have; and harsh experience will already have given them many of the answers expressed here — without the aid of any textbook. They may also have encountered other problems and solutions that have been missed. I would much appreciate hearing from them, and in as much detail as possible — suggestions, experiences, case histories, illustrative anecdotes, repercussions, even disasters; for the official neglect that has shrouded this whole area (in contrast to the personal concern of many practitioners) can only have spawned its share of disaster. Many such catastrophes have been narrowly averted by prompt, efficient common-sense, and the experienced responses of doctors and nurses to some of the problems set out below. I would be happy to become a focus for further, more detailed and illustrated research into this subject.

The lack of published sources was, in the end, more than compensated by the wealth of material that was so generously offered in response to the enquiries and questionnaires that were distributed. Some contributors had obviously gone to the trouble of researching their replies, despite being experts in their own fields. In sum, the contributions were of such a value that the scope of the work has expanded far beyond its intended relevance to nurses, doctors, midwives, paramedical staff and ambulance crews to include community social workers, voluntary workers of all kinds, sociologists and students in the social sciences. It may also appeal to members of the general public who have developed an interest in other religions and cultures or who need to understand them for professional or social reasons. The essence of a culture or belief is often expressed in its attitudes to life and death and to health, sickness and pain. That is what this book is all about. I hope that my formal acknowledgement will succeed in conveying the depth of my gratitude to all contributors.

Although it seems inappropriate to concentrate on the problems involved in putting the principles discussed in this book into practice (indeed it would take a book in itself) the reader is urged to consider the institutional obstacle — bureaucratic, organizational, or political — that can arise when any new approach is implemented.

If these harsh realities are not faced, the aspects of care outlined in this book risk being neglected while patients from differing religions and cultures contend with insensitivity to, and ignorance of, their particular needs.

A. C. M. Sampson

ACKNOWLEDGEMENTS

This book could not have been written without the help and support of many individuals and organizations. All the opinions and comments are my own, however, and none of those who have helped can be held responsible for the way in which I have presented the information they so generously gave me.

For factual information about various religions and religious groups I am indebted to Miss Carolyn Halhed; the Most Reverend Metropolitan Anthony of Sourozh, of the Russian Orthodox Church; the Revd Canon Eric Reid, Secretary and Director of Training, Hospital Chaplaincies Council; the Revd Richard J. Hamper, General Secretary, and Revd D. M. Main, Secretary of the Hospital Chaplaincies Board, Free Church Federal Council; Captain Paul A. du Plessis, Medical Adviser, The Salvation Army; Mrs Myra Hutchinson, Chaplain's Assistant, Western General Hospital, Edinburgh; Mr George H. Gorman, General Secretary, the Religious Society of Friends (Quakers); Revd Richard J. Hall, Secretary, London Congregational Union Inc; Mr Brian McEvoy, Catholic Enquiry Centre; Mr B. K. Chandari, Secretary, India Society of Sheffield; Mr A. A. Shamis, Muslim Information Services; Rabbi Julia Neuberger, South London Liberal Synagogue; The Public Communications Department, Church of Jesus Christ of Latter Day Saints, London; Mr Richard Robinson, District Manager, Christian Science Committee on Publications; Mr David Sibney, Public Relations Officer, Watch Tower Bible and Tract Society of Pennsylvania (British Isles Branch); Mr T. M. Johnson, Secretary, Spiritualist Association of Great Britain; Revd Sydney Knight, London Unitarian District Minister, Miss Michele Pinto and Miss Sharon Cavanagh, Department of Medical Social Work, St Mary's Hospital, London; and the World Congress of Faiths.

There were numerous other individuals who gave me their time and kindness but they prefer to remain anonymous for personal or religious reasons. I am grateful to them for their advice and support.

On cultural matters I received valuable help from many people, but I should particularly like to thank Miss Marlene Hinchelwood of the Commission for Racial Equality, Miss Alix Hindley and the Community Relations Councils in Blackburn, Camden, Lothian, Manchester, Sheffield and Tayside. I am also grateful to the staff of several Embassies, High Commissions, and Consulates who provided information. I should also like to thank Mrs Jenny Storer and the editor of the *Journal of Human Nutrition* for permission to quote from Mrs Storer's work on page 28.

Many friends and colleagues gave up time to discuss, criticize, and add inspiration. I cannot name them all but I would like to thank Professor A. T. Altschul, the Revd Dr A. V. Campbell and the Revd T. Stewart McGregor in particular. When I had just begun to look into this subject they listened to me and with their early encouragement this book became possible. They have helped me since by reading, criticizing, and challenging. If anything has slipped in unchallenged, it is my fault and not theirs. Throughout the writing of this book I have had considerable moral support and personal encouragement from Major General C. E. Eberhardie and Mrs Mary Chapple. To Mary I am also indebted for the title.

No author could have received more kindness, patience, and good humour than I have from Miss Kay Baxter of McGraw-Hill; and the manuscript would never have seen the light of day if my former secretary, Mrs Elizabeth Marnham, had not typed it!

Finally, I wish to thank the many patients, families and colleagues of varying nationalities, cultures and creeds who have taught me so much (and are still teaching me) and to whom this book is dedicated.

A. C. M. Sampson

AUTHOR'S NOTE

In terminology, I have often preferred the popular to the strictly accurate word. To be pedantic, the words doctor, nurse, midwife, health visitor, ambulanceman, physiotherapist, radiotherapist, occupational therapist, speech therapist, radiographer, hospital technician, psychologist, psychotherapist, remedial gymnast, social worker, minister of religion and voluntary worker would occur so often as to make the book unreadable. Therefore, I have had to resort constantly to collective words. Since the relevant group is different in almost every context, accurate collective nouns do not exist to describe them. So I have been forced to use expressions such as 'hospital professions' or 'hospital community' to describe groups which are, in fact, as numerous outside hospitals as they are within them! The same applies to the more concise expression 'staff'. Group terms such as 'paramedical staff', 'social worker' and 'therapist' have had to be used in the loosest possible sense. Sometimes I have used the word 'practitioner' which must be taken, like all my other terms, to include anyone who is relevant to the context.

Where, for variety, I have named doctors, nurses, midwives, etc. (and I have also dispensed with tiresome repetition of 'etc.') the list is not intended to be exclusive in its context. Sometimes I have named just doctors and nurses in the same sense. Adjectives such as 'medical' and 'nursing' are used in the same loose way as in 'medical and nursing ethics'. The term 'ethical norm' has been used to describe the ethical codes of practice which are normal throughout the 'hospital professions' in Britain, as they are applied to patients from ethnic groups and religions indigenous to these islands. 'Ethical variations' is used to describe those variations from the ethical norms which must be considered when dealing with patients from other religions and cultures. The term 'midwife' has been retained because some are still practising who are not also nurses, while the term 'nurse' often includes those now trained as midwives.

In Britain the hospital chaplain is an important focus when matters of conscience arise; and he is often needed as a point of contact with ministers of other religions whether they are indigenous here or not. But since the term 'chaplain' refers strictly only to the Anglican, Free and Roman Catholic Churches, I have avoided using the word, except where it is both accurate and necessary to do so, in favour of 'minister of religion' or simply 'minister', which can be used safely in any context.

Discrimination between the sexes

In a book on such a subject as this, it is impracticable to eliminate completely the use of genders and retain a fluent and readable text. The reader is asked to accept that any deliberate distinction between the sexes is not implied.

1. INTRODUCTION AND THEORETICAL BACKGROUND

General scope

The 'neglected ethic' I refer to is described in the International Council of Nurses (ICN) *Code of Nursing Ethics* as follows:

> The nurse, in providing care, promotes an environment in which the values, customs and spiritual beliefs of the individual are respected.

Nurses do not *deliberately* neglect the customs and spiritual beliefs of their patients; in general, they are much too badly informed in this area to do anything deliberately. This is bad enough, in all conscience, even today. But a keynote of this book is the theme of change and the challenge of the future. In the past patients were usually cared for by nurses and doctors from their own area, and who had lived and practised in the same regions all their lives. Often a nurse would have travelled only to the nearest city or to the capital. Nowadays, nurses, doctors and patients may be from different cities, regions, countries, religions and cultures. Somehow they must meet the challenge of understanding each other first, before attempting to anticipate the needs of patients who come from different ethnic backgrounds. This leads at once to the realm beyond the nursing profession to that of both nursing and medical training, to include training in all the paramedical professions – for ethics recognize no divisions nor frontiers.

Ethics and the dangers of 'playing God'

In acute emergency, dire consequences have often been deflected by doctors in particular, taking the law into their own hands based upon their own judgement and interpretation of the best interests of the patients, and damning the cultural and religious consequences and the implicit or explicit wishes of the patients or family. Usually this has shown courage, sometimes ignorance and occasionally an insensitive arrogance. Hospital staff have their full share of human virtues and failings. It is no use warning of the dangers of 'playing God'. In the metaphorical sense in which this term is now coming to be used, those who must shoulder responsibility for resuscitating the 'dead', transfusing blood into the living, injecting potentially lethal or mind-bending drugs, terminating pregnancies and handling teenage contraception, performing dangerous surgery, transplanting human and animal tissues, inserting mechanical parts into humans, and all too often having to switch off life-support systems – all these utterly fallible people have no honourable way of shirking what comes to be an unavoidable duty; however distressing or traumatic the task may be. The doctors, nurses, midwives and ambulance crews who have to perform these functions are trained in the technical procedures involved and are supported morally by an ethical code of practice that has grown up around them *as it applies to patients of their own culture and main religious groupings*. These ethical codes of practice, which are already well researched and documented, and which are referred to as 'ethical norms' are neither formulated nor defined here.

Ethical variations

It is the variations from the norm that must be considered when dealing with patients from other religions and cultures; these ethical variations should be applied *where necessary*. The ethical norms become a point of departure, with the ethical variations as an added dimension, and both require application of the same care, sensitivity and conscience, and the same degree of consultation — where appropriate and feasible — although of course the decision-making group concerned will vary with the cultural and religious factors involved. So, because ethical variations are an extension of ethical norms, it is important to say something about the latter, especially as the extension will *not necessarily be in a straight line*. But these remarks are confined to general observations affecting *all* ethical problems, such as the general attitudes, circumstances and atmosphere which surround them, and the problem of training staff in handling the interrelationship of ethical, medical and nursing judgements. As already stated the ethical norms themselves should already be familiar to hospital practitioners.

Consultation, decision-making and family involvement

One general point that applies both to familiar ethical norms and to cultural and religious variations is that vital decisions are not made without agonized discussion and soul-searching within the responsible group, where appropriate and if time permits. The composition of the group will vary but may include one or more doctors and nurses, a minister of religion and members of the patient's family. The latter are often omitted, either because the technicalities of the decision prevent them making a contribution; or because a dangerously emotional decision might lead to avoidable suffering; or because the case is such that it would be cruel to the family to involve them in sharing a decision which can only be more agonizing for them than it is for those who are trained and practiced in preserving their professional and clinical judgement.

While many practitioners and the lay public believe that the family should *always* be consulted, and they have a right to their opinion, the consensus of experienced practitioners is overwhelmingly against this (the argument here, remember, is that the family should *always* be consulted as an exclusive right). In fact, families often do not wish to be consulted, or are grateful that the decision has been made without them by those whom they believe are best qualified to judge, although invariably they appreciate the reassurance that every available recourse has been exhausted before a bitter decision becomes irrevocable. Where bereavement follows they usually do not wish to know any of the unpleasant details but always appreciate any reassurance that the end was, in fact, inevitable and that it occurred without suffering and with the minimum of anxiety and discomfort. Usually they wish to be present, and this should be arranged wherever possible in the most dignified and sympathetic way that can be managed in the circumstances. Variations in terminal care and arrangements, last offices and the involvement of families in these situations are dealt with as fully as possible below.

Unfair responsibility, neglect and their effects

Sometimes, for technical or practical reasons, vital decisions must be made quickly and alone, usually by a doctor, but often by a nurse, midwife or ambulance crew. Tragically, they must sometimes be taken alone, or in a small group, by staff who are forced by circumstances to act beyond their competence — and who know it. However, a positive outcome is that these situations often bring out what is courageous and best in all branches of the hospital community, and form the making or breaking point in a practitioner's training and experience.

Because of understaffing, even nursing students sometimes find themselves, most unfairly, in the position where a patient collapses suddenly and unexpectedly. By way of reassuring lay public and patients, it may be added that the whole nature of illness and trauma, including sudden accidents in homes and streets, and sometimes remote areas, makes these situations unavoidable. If there is anything to be done, it lies in the hands of those who would be better employed improving the pay and working conditions of hospital staff to prevent disillusionment and wastage, and in the better allocation and management of resources, than in 'back-seat driving' the hospital professions. The chief fault within the hospital community itself lies in the tendency of practitioners, including some of the best, not to interest themselves sufficiently in administrative and professional matters that lie outside their own specializations. So these inevitably fall increasingly into the hands of lay administrators, outside bodies, 'do-gooders' and politicians, who should not automatically be made the scapegoats of our own neglect. This applies in all areas from the organization of the NHS down to the training of staff in the identification and handling of ethical problems.

Culture and religious reactions to new procedures

Beyond the ethical practices which surround our own cultural and religious groupings lie the extra factors that must be superimposed upon them to allow for the customs and taboos, the spiritual needs and fears and psychological makeup of the less understood cultural and religious groups. Above, it was implied that crucial judgements are made, often successfully, by practitioners who are following their own clinical judgement and native ethical code in either ignorance or defiance of the unfamiliar mentality with which they are faced. Many of the critical procedures in question are fairly new, of western origin and little understood even by our own relatively educated public. But patients from another culture, probably less scientifically aware and often centred thousands of miles away, may have little or no idea of what is really happening or being done to them; nor may their families. It is possible, quite literally, to get away with murder — or what is murder in the eyes of the group concerned and in a form that is abhorrent to them. In some cases there has not yet been time for cultural or religious attitudes to form or harden around new procedures.

Change and the future

Of course, this will change, in time; it is changing already. The wonders of modern medicine and hospital care make big headlines and are beamed all over the world on transistor-cheapened and rapidly proliferating radios and satellite-relayed television. Yesterday's obscure wonder is becoming today's common knowledge — even to children. So today's practitioner cannot now avoid, even if he would, developing a more sensitive understanding of the ethical concerns of others if, at best, he is to practise with optimum efficiency, and at worst, to avoid plunging himself and his hospital into scandal and recrimination, which could be worse if the cause is racial. For those who may feel that this is an exaggeration, it would be as well to remember that the final spark which ignited the Indian Mutiny in 1857 was the need for Indian soldiers to bite off cartridges coated with animal grease, which, whether it came from cows or pigs, was bound to offend both Hindus and Muslims.

The future looms, exciting but forbidding. Science has passed through a series of revolutions. We have seen the industrial revolution, the mechanical revolution culminating in the aeroplane, the nuclear revolution, the space revolution, and now we are in the middle of the electronic revolution. It is in the nature of scientific change to proceed by geometrical rather than arithmetical progression, as each new wonder matures in an ever-shortening time-scale. There is general agreement among scientists that we are already into the next stage — the biological revolution. This includes more than the radical developments such as transplant surgery, immunology, recent advances in drugs, nuclear medicine and radiotherapy or life-support systems. All these, which have already raised some resounding ethical questions, preceded the biological revolution proper, which began with the cracking of the DNA molecular code and the consequent synthesis of new life-forms. The ethical questions arising out of genetic engineering and all its possible implications are staggering and, while all this goes far beyond the scope of this book, some perspective is needed, at a time of such dynamic change, as a framework for the present.

Future dangers and a two-tier solution

The specific point made above is that ethical factors will become *more* complex and compelling, not less so. And, after making a sluggish start in this field, there is no time to lose. Nor can these matters remain the exclusive prerogative of the medical, nursing and allied professions. Public disquiet is already evident, if not yet widespread, and scientists, sociologists, religious and other institutions, politicians and governments will become increasingly involved. Legislation has begun and must inevitably proliferate. All these developments may well be right; certainly they are unavoidable. But they bring new dangers in their wake, that follow from tying the hands and narrowing the options of those who must continue to bear the real responsibilities; and who appreciate only too well the difficulties and dangers of defining too closely, let alone in writing the limits to be set upon actions and procedures. Hence the development of unwritten ethical codes of practice within the hospital community, which must in turn realize the extent of the burden it is assuming, as the ethical problems and choices multiply and become more complex.

A two-tier process seems to be developing whereby the longer established and publicized procedures first become common knowledge and of general concern, then subject to public debate and finally, and hopefully very selectively, to legislation. Meanwhile the hospital community tries to hold its course, picking its way through new legislation, trying to apply it in a practical way to newly arising problems, and continuing to exercise its own conscience and judgement where the edges do not fit. This makes sense, so long as a correct balance between the hospital professions, public and government can be maintained. For this to happen, the hospital professions must retain the confidence of the public and of parliament, and this confidence can only be earned and deserved if consciences, minds and talents are increasingly addressed to these areas of justifiable public concern.

Ethical factors in routine practice

It is not intended for this book to give the impression that all decisions containing ethical judgements are grand, vital and heroic ones, nor that only these are important. The psychosomatic element in recovery from almost all disease, and from much physical trauma, is common knowledge. What is not so commonly known is the high percentage figure that is given to it, as a factor in recovery, by many leading doctors. In relating cultural and ethical factors to these psychosomatic effects it may be observed that such tolerances vary widely in racial and cultural groupings, and that some of those powers of resistance and recuperation which can be most quickly and adversely affected are found in some of the important minorities in Britain. By a quirk of nature, some of these same minorities can also be the most heavily influenced by an authoritarian environment.

A NON-CONSTRUCTIVE ILLUSTRATION

To illustrate the combined effect of just these two observations in a routine, rather than heroic, situation imagine, say, a female patient who speaks adequate but not good English, who has lived her entire life either among her own people or, more recently, as an immigrant, within an enclave of her own kind in a large city. She is taken into hospital seriously but not critically ill. Her own culture is strongly hierarchical and authoritarian and, even within these general constraints, the man is always the decision-maker; it is not for a woman to question his authority or his judgements. His word is law. She is weak and confused by her illness and, as she looks around her in a general hospital ward, she sees disciplined rows of beds with uniformed nurses going about their business in what seems to her a brisk and authoritarian fashion, however kind and gentle they may be.

An unconscious patient is wheeled into the ward, a trolley goes by gleaming with equipment and tubes and dials; a curtain is pulled around the ensemble from which emanate some rhythmic, mechanical and, to her, frightening noises of powerful suction interrupted by violent coughing and retching. A sinister group of white-coated men appear with stethoscopes around their necks followed by more starched, uniformed and forbidding females bearing charts and pushing another trolley, laden this time with glass and metal beakers, drugs and instruments. They move purposefully and systematically around the ward and begin to approach her bed. She sees a male doctor apparently exploring with his hands the neck, shoulders and chest of another woman patient — an act that is strictly forbidden by her religion and culture, and totally repugnant to her. She has not yet seen her family since she arrived in an ambulance, she feels she is in a totally hostile environment cut off from her people, culture and kin. The poor woman is terrified even before a hand has been laid upon her, any treatment has begun, nor any of her specific sensitivities violated. In her terror she attempts to pray, and gropes helplessly for her religious books and symbols that normally comfort her in moments of stress. Since she is of a race and culture that does not usually recuperate quickly and strongly, it is hard to imagine a worse psychosomatic background for subsequent treatment. Even when she has gathered her wits and been somewhat reassured by the kindness and gentleness of the doctors and nurses, she may still feel too subdued or embarrassed to ask for the religious symbols she craves (let alone argue against treatment that is disapproved of by her culture — until the wrath of her husband descends upon her for permitting it!)

A CONSTRUCTIVE ILLUSTRATION

By contrast, now imagine the same case but with an experienced nurse who, when taking the nursing history on admission, notes at once the race and religion of the patient. The curtains are drawn to screen off frightening distractions, and after some skilful and understanding questioning, the nurse draws out of the patient any problems she may have. After being reassured, if possible, about her condition, she should be told that she can be examined by a female doctor if she insists. She is then asked if she would like any specific religous symbols together with anything else she treasures. She is told straightaway about visiting times, and that after she has been examined arrangements can be made for her to see the dietician about dietary restrictions imposed by her religion. If there is a portable telephone, she can telephone her family and, if not, they can be contacted and asked to bring with them anything she needs.

Quite apart from the pre-emptive attack on fear and clinical shock which these simple but knowledgeable measures portend, and beyond the therapeutic effects of the general reassurance they contain, they cannot fail to engender *confidence* or at least relative confidence in the hospital environment and in the knowledge and expertise of the medical and nursing staff. Since confidence in the efficacy of treatment is a prime ingredient of psychosomatic therapy and, assuming that all aspects of medical treatment and patient care are handled with the same knowledge, skill and tact, the ultimate recovery of the patient can hardly fail to benefit from the nurse's expertise. This is written both in the hope of engendering more of the latter-style scenarios and fewer of the first, and in the hope that it may become a first general textbook on the subject to promote systematic training and further research that will lead, in turn, to the better and more comprehensive care of the patients and to the greater confidence and solace of their families, whether anxious or bereaved.

In contrast to this first introductory chapter on the general and theoretical aspects of the subject, with its wider perspectives and its future, the following three chapters deal with the basic ingredients of understanding in the fields of culture and religion.

2. A GENERAL APPROACH TO RELIGIOUS AND CULTURAL FACTORS

The handling of cultural and religious differences can be divided into general categories arising out of:
1. Increased travel on business or holiday.
2. Immigration.
3. Nurses' and doctors' own beliefs and emotions.
4. Modern developments in medicine and surgery.
5. The needs patients have in common.

Increased travel on business or holiday

Mass travel, sometimes over great distances, is vastly increasing the numbers of patients who fall ill away from home. All over the world there are people arriving at airports, in strange cities and staying in hotels in towns or countries that are alien to them. Such a patient may find it difficult to communicate because first-aiders, nurses, doctors and others involved in his care may not understand his language or dialect. This may add to his feeling of being in a hostile environment where there is little understanding of his values, religion or culture.

For example, a Japanese businessman leaves Tokyo and within 36 hours he has collapsed at London Airport. He is taken to a hospital where, although he knows a little English, he may return to using his native language because he is confused about his condition. He will long not only for his homeland, family and friends but also for the customs, values and beliefs which go with them. He may be a Buddhist and, because he is forced to rest, he may use the time to reflect on the meaning of his life or wish to read from Buddhist literature.

If he is totally unaccustomed to the British way of life, he will probably long for meals to be cooked and served in the Japanese way. He will be offended by the use of his first name and the absence of formality. All this should be taken into account, and wherever practically possible these needs should be met. The assistance of the Japanese embassy can be sought.

Immigration

Individuals who have come from one culture and have chosen to live permanently in another, for whatever reason, have different needs from those of the person who collapses in another country while on a temporary visit.

For example, a young Asian whose family has emigrated to Britain may have parents who were brought up in one culture, whereas he is being educated in Britain. His values, customs and beliefs may be in a state of change; his life at school or work may differ from that at home. Caring for this patient requires great understanding, and the nurse must take into consideration the values, beliefs and customs of the patient's friends and relatives. Sometimes she may find herself acting as a buffer between the two cultures. While not taking sides, she can use her position to emphasize the clinical priority, which may be in danger of being submerged under emotional factors.

Nurses' and doctors' own beliefs and emotions

It is essential for those in the hospital team, who are not indigenous to the area, to understand and tolerate the values, customs and beliefs of the country and region in which they are working; and this must be done regardless of personal feelings and dislikes. Racial, cultural and religious matters can arouse strong personal feelings and distastes, which may have a psychological or physical basis, and the hospital community is not immune to them. To those nursing students who are seized with the romance of doing good to mankind it must, in fairness, be said that much of it is far from glamorous although a marvellous challenge. Unless one feels strongly enough about it to overcome all personal distastes in the interests of the patients and their families *as a matter of routine* — and this goes for all racial, cultural and religious distastes — then it would be better to forget about nursing and take up a totally different profession.

Modern developments in medicine and surgery

The problems created by recent developments in medical and surgical practice, and the biological revolution to come, have already been mentioned. But to the more spectacular aspects such as organ transplants, spare part surgery, resuscitating the apparently dead and in other ways prolonging life, must be added more everyday aspects such as birth control, terminating pregnancies, administering new drugs and other clinical innovations for curing or preventing disease. Each new development can have implications for the patient's personal values, his culture and religious beliefs. All too often, of course, he will not consider them until he is ill or, alternatively, his next of kin may have to face them on his behalf. The problems are aggravated if the staff have not considered the implications themselves prior to the occurrence of a difficult situation or sudden emergency.

For example, Mr G, an Orthodox Jew, has been suffering from diabetes for twelve years and was treated entirely with insulin. A new government regulation obliged the drug company manufacturing his particular form of insulin to specify on the packet the source of the insulin. In this way Mr G discovers that he has been on porcine insulin for twelve years. His reaction is one of complete revulsion; his attitudes toward, and his respect for, the medical and nursing staff who have been caring for him, change at once. He no longer trusts them and feels he has been deceived. The nurses and doctors have failed to appreciate that an orthodox Jew may not ingest anything that has come from a pig, in any form whatsoever.

The needs patients have in common

If the patient is to be understood, nurses and doctors must first differentiate between normal and abnormal behaviour. Before labelling the patient's behaviour abnormal the nurse should discover if there are any social, cultural and religious factors to be taken into consideration. Injury or illness, especially in the case of sudden illness or accident, often provoke patients into questioning the purpose and quality of their lives, asking the nurse perhaps 'Why did this happen to me?' Patients' relatives and close friends may also require help and comfort at this time, for they too may be questioning the reason for the patient's suffering, especially when the patient has a painful, disfiguring or fatal illness, or has been severely or fatally injured in an accident.

The patient may not previously have given much thought to the purpose of his life or to any spiritual or religious beliefs. So he may suddenly find himself thinking about such matters for the first time. He may perceive the accident or illness to be a punishment for having done something sinful, or for having failed to do something he considers right. He may wish to express his anxieties to a minister of the religion that he was brought up to practice or into which he was initiated. The nurse should know straight away where she can locate such a minister.

For example, Miss M, a Roman Catholic, is admitted to hospital following a ruptured posterior communicating artery aneurysm. She has a complete hemiplegia and is very distressed. She regards her illness as a punishment from God for having taken oral contraceptives.

General discussion

Below is a brief overview of some specific aspects of care which may be influenced by social, cultural and religious factors. These factors are first discussed in general terms, and in Parts 3 and 4 are considered in more detail and in relation to particular religions and sects.

Basic beliefs

It is unrealistic to expect *every* nurse and doctor to be an expert on every religion and sect. But they should familiarize themselves with the basics of the major religions and the significant differences between the various religious sects. National characteristics, cultural factors and strong political beliefs can intermingle with and colour these basics, and may distort or even apparently extinguish them — which puts an increased burden upon the sensitivity and understanding of the practitioner. To confuse the issue still further, the religious beliefs of childhood, which have long been submerged under strong political convictions, may return to make a very powerful challenge, if only in the form of doubt, in cases of serious illnesses, trauma or approaching death. It may be in the interests of both patients and staff if patients of actively opposing religions or political views are separated if they appear to be causing a disturbance or if their treatment is adversely affected. It is also advisable to know the name of the religious book(s) of each major religion — for example, the Holy Bible, the Koran and the Torah or Talmud.

Religious observances

Each religion has its own particular observances. First, there is usually an initiation into the religion, such as baptism; then, there is generally a series of special festivals in the year, such as the Christian Easter, Jewish Passover and the Muslim Ramadhan. Each religion also has its own religious articles such as prayer shawls, beads, rosaries, crucifixes, etc. The nurse has to be careful to respect such articles and to provide conditions in which an individual or group of patients can practise their religion without being disturbed, and without disturbing others.

Clothing

Many religions and sects have particular views about clothing. For example, a Sikh man wears a turban. Some Muslim women wear long black garments (*chador*) and, in some countries, the whole body except for the eyes is covered.

Nurses should also be aware of the patient's attitude to being undressed. As shown below, many religions are very strict about who can undress a person of that religion. In some, an unmarried woman cannot undress a man, and a man may not undress a woman; in other cases a person of a different sect or religion may not see the person naked — in some sects the person is never allowed to be totally naked, and has to wear an article of clothing at all times, even in the bath (for instance, pants or a small cap).

The body

Apart from clothing, a patient may be particularly sensitive about exposing his body or parts of it but, in addition, may have other particular taboos about certain parts of the body.

To give a few examples: hair is particularly important in some religions, the most obvious examples being the Sikhs and the Orthodox Jews. In some faiths a woman is not allowed to expose her breasts or genitalia to a man other than her husband, unless her husband gives his permission. If the husband does not give his consent, then the patient must be examined by a female doctor.

In some Middle Eastern countries, food may be touched with only one hand (see page 36). To use the other hand is considered unclean as that hand is used for cleaning the perineum after defaecation. Imagine the problems that result when such a patient has one hand encased in plaster! Care of the body after death is discussed in various sections on last offices see Part 4.

Diet

Religion and culture can strongly influence an individual's diet. Even patients who are not particularly religious frequently retain the diet of that religion either out of habit or for social reasons. Conversely, some patients may be very strict about certain observances but not about others, diet included.

For example, many Roman Catholics still do not eat meat on Fridays, even though the rule forbidding this was waived many years ago, and now applies officially only to certain days in the church's calendar.

Some Anglicans as well as Roman Catholics fast before taking Holy Communion although this is not essential for them. In some religions, believers are *expected* to fast during certain festivals — Jews and Muslims have special festivals during which they *must* do so (Yom Kippur and Ramadhan).

Nurses and doctors must remember that if a particular food or animal is taboo, then it is forbidden in *every* way. If the patient is not to eat pork, he must not have pig in *any* form; this means no bacon, ham or other foodstuffs which contain ham or bacon, or any drugs which come from pig tissue. Patients who do not speak English find difficulty in understanding the instructions on food packets; they may be misled and eat a forbidden food or mistakenly refuse foods believing them to contain forbidden ingredients.

For example, in one urban clinic the health visitors noticed that some mothers among the Asian community were not feeding their babies the powdered milk that they had been given (Cow and Gate). It was discovered that, because the packet had a picture of a cow on it, the mothers were convinced that the contents came from dead cows. The cow is a sacred animal to Hindus, although they are allowed to drink its milk.

Many patients from abroad have difficulties in hospital because they are not accustomed to a British diet. A nurse must also as a clinical necessity, differentiate between a patient with a true loss of appetite, or a dislike for the food offered, and one who eats frugally.

Drugs or alcohol

Many patients may refuse drugs for religious or cultural reasons. (Pain-relieving drugs are dealt with under 'pain'.) Some of the drugs most frequently refused are tranquillizers, sedatives and hypnotics. Restrictions on the use of alcohol are found in many religions, and in several of the religions and sects it is completely forbidden.

Pain

The response of a patient is very complex. One has many factors to consider not least among them being culture and religion. Take, for example, the 'stiff upper lip' image of the British, the importance of 'face' to the Japanese, or the more expressive response of those from some Mediterranean countries. It is particularly important to understand these differences, which can seriously affect diagnosis and treatment, and they are dealt with below in more detail.

Treatment

To make the assumption that a patient agrees to treatment when he is brought into hospital is dangerous especially if, when he was fit, he believed that it was wrong to consent to surgical or medical intervention. In such cases, medical, nursing and other hospital team members are presented with a very serious dilemma. The most publicized cases in recent years in Britain have been those in which parents who are Jehovah's Witnesses refused to allow doctors to give their children blood transfusions. There are others, of course, and they present many of the most difficult moral dilemmas in medicine today. Antibiotic therapy, termination of pregnancy, contraception, replacement and spare part surgery, organ transplantation, resuscitation and the prolongation of life are all issues which have been at the centre of medical moral dilemmas, some throughout the ages and others in the wake of scientific advance. Religion and culture play a vital role in trying to resolve these dilemmas.

All too seldom doctors and nurses are faced with alternatives that are good or bad. All too often their choice lies between alternatives that are bad or worse. In such cases the problem is often compounded because it is difficult or impossible to distinguish between what is bad or worse; so experience, professional instinct and flair become the only guide. Group analysis and discussion helps, when practicable, so long as it is confined to those who share the responsibility.

Terminal care

When a person is dying his thoughts turn to his life, its meaning, and to what will happen to him in the future. He may reflect on whether he will ever see his family and loved ones again, either in this world or the next. Someone who has already thought this through and has become a firm believer in a particular religious faith may wish to be visited by his minister of religion, to receive the rites and offices of his religion. A Roman Catholic, for example, who is seriously ill will be offered the 'last rites' of the church (more correctly called the 'Sacrament of the Sick') in the hope that his life may be spared or, if he dies, that his soul will be blessed.

In some religions the family or persons appointed by the minister of religion must wail beside the patient's bed. This is uncommon in Britain and creates difficulties in open wards. It presents a challenge to nursing staff to provide an environment in which these rites may be carried out without disturbing other patients. It is easier to manage in a patient's home.

The careful management of these religious observances can allow a patient to die with dignity, and reassure his relatives that he was not only offered physical and mental solace but spiritual comfort too.

Last offices

At the time of death the nurse should take into account any religious rites and taboos concerning the patient's body. In some religions the nurse can perform this last duty for a patient with respect and dignity. In other cases, however, the nurse must not touch the body at all. The bodies of Jewish patients, for instance, must not be touched by anyone other than a Jewish *mohel*, or, according to the Jewish faith, his soul will be adversely affected.

Relationships with other people

In many cultures, women are not permitted to make decisions. For instance, they are not allowed to sign their own consent forms for treatment or surgery; a husband or brother has to do it for them. Also, a Muslim woman is only allowed to wash a man if she cannot be considered eligible to marry him. In some Christian sects (Plymouth or other Brethren), members of the sect are not permitted to sit down to meals with those who are not members of the same sect, nor can they socialize with them. This may lead to misunderstanding in the ward if the nurse is not aware of such practices. Attitudes to marriage, birth, children, the elderly and the handicapped also differ in many faiths and cultures, and all these are covered in Parts 3 and 4.

3. SOME CULTURAL ASPECTS OF CARE OF PATIENTS

This part is arranged in the form of an alphabetical index.

When looking at the cultures of patients, it is important to find a working definition of culture because it is a term widely used in many different contexts, some of them inapplicable to the care of patients. The health care team has to look at the historical, religious and social background of the region and/or country from which the patient and his family originate. Often the patient was born in one country, and his parents in another, so the culture in which the patient was educated must also be taken into account. This may bring in yet a third culture!

Tradition, history, folklore, national and regional customs all play their part in the makeup of a person's cultural background, as do politics, economics and geography. Subcultures within a culture also develop and bring about further changes in the culture as a whole. Doctors and nurses, in particular, need to be sensitive to the culture, and if possible the subculture, of the catchment area of the hospital or community district in which they work. The health care team can then respond in an understanding way to the emotional, social and physical needs of the patients, and possibly find solutions to any anxieties the patient may have by identifying the real problem. The roots of this may have escaped him completely, since he has been too close to their causes to recognize them, whether they be the result of family, social or cultural pressures, or conflict, great or small, between two cultures to which he has been exposed, or between a subculture and its parent form.

The pressures involved in such cases may be overt, hidden or merely potential. The emotional pressures are always real to the person involved but they may be lessened or even completely overcome by a clearer understanding of the real underlying pressures and tensions involved. Often the individual's perception of a pressure has no real basis, and sensitive staff can help by quietly working through the problem or discussing it with the patient.

The hospital can be a place of change and integration or, as Michael Wilson put it in his book of the same title, 'a place of truth'. Its primary objective is the diagnosis, treatment and care of the sick but, fortunately it can also become an environment in which some understanding and integration between cultures, creeds and classes takes place.

Individuals react differently to their fellow patients, to staff and to the institution itself. They are inevitably vulnerable, anxious and uncertain, and these feelings frequently bring together people who may never meet in other circumstances, let alone speak to each other, and a relationship will develop for the space of a few hours or days. But this very mingling of cultures can also accentuate a patient's feeling of isolation when he is far from home, family, friends and perhaps his own native culture. Many of the habits, customs and people he has taken for granted may now be missed acutely and he may long for them in a way which often seems disproportionate to an impartial observer.

Some patients who have come from other cultures or live within a family from another group, may find their arrival in hospital not only a time of possible friction but also when different aspects of the two cultures come sharply into focus. This may lead either to mental conflict or, conversely, to clarification and to therapeutic peace of mind. For those caring for the patient in his own home, the cultural focus lies within the home and family. As a member of the primary care team is a guest in the patient's home, it becomes all the more difficult to give the proper care required without offending cultural sensibilities, and even greater tact and sensitivity than usual may be required, together with some firmness. The cultural environment in which treatment takes place may be totally different from that of the practitioner; indeed, practitioner and patient may be from two groups which differ again from the indigenous population, for example, an Asian patient being treated by a West Indian doctor in a London suburb. A patient's vulnerability is less marked in the familiar surroundings of his own home.

The nurse's role is to minimize anxiety, to be aware of potential conflicts but not to create them. By careful observation she should pick up signs of anxiety or difficulty in the patient, which may be cultural or religious in origin. She should be able both to sidestep problems, and to deal with them realistically as appropriate, and practically.

The practical aspect should be stressed because trying to accommodate all the cultural needs and desires of all patients all the time can be impractical and unrealistic and may even cause more problems than it solves. Sometimes both patient and staff must compromise in order to reach an acceptable outcome. Trying to meet the individual needs of a patient is one of the most exciting aspects of nursing care. All that this part of the book offers is a few pointers, suggestions and material for reflection. It does not pretend to be comprehensive.

Alcohol

In some countries, particularly in western society, a myth exists that if a man does not drink alcohol and if, in addition, he cannot drink a lot of alcohol without becoming drunk, he is weak and 'not really a man'. This attitude can be quite easily seen in the United Kingdom, Eire, in many countries of mainland Europe, in the United States, and in the USSR. Until recently this was the theme of alcohol advertising in the United Kingdom.

Sometimes a patient may deliberately mislead a doctor by either understating or overstating his drinking habits; a patient, assuming that the doctor will disapprove of his drinking habits, understates them but, in trying to impress the nurse, he may overstate them! This may be totally inconsequential and cause only mild amusement, but fear of admitting that he or she drinks may lead a patient who has a serious drinking problem to try to hide it — along with a supply of bottles in the bedside locker!

Some patients come from countries where alcohol is completely forbidden. Very severe punishments have been reported for those who try to smuggle alcohol into strict Muslim countries such as Iraq, Iran and Saudi Arabia. To offer alcohol to such a patient in any digestible form, either orally as a drink or parenterally may cause religious and cultural offence to such a patient. On the other hand, the patient may accept alcohol either because it is prescribed as a medicine or because he is tempted to take the opportunity to drink now that he has a valid excuse. In either case, if he is unused to it the effects may be accentuated.

Nurses should take care to ensure that patients who refuse alcohol altogether on grounds of religion or conscience do not inadvertently receive it. For example, some medicines have an alcohol base as in some strong pain-relieving mixtures. Some patients may even be suspicious of the use of chlorhexidine in spirit and other skin cleansing agents.

Bereavement

The distinct phases of bereavement are handled differently in various regional and cultural groups. In Britain, for example, one tends to find a 'stiff upper lip' type of response during which the bereaved individual, particularly if he is a man, will do almost anything rather than be seen to cry. Many of those who cry and express their grief openly try to hide it, apologize for it and feel embarrassed by it. For these people privacy is essential. They must be allowed to be alone or with their family and friends away from the stares of others. The nurse and other health care workers can be most helpful in providing a quiet, understanding and listening role. The nurse must help the family to express its grief in its own way without being embarrassed. At this time words sometimes appear inadequate but letting the person hold her hand, cry on her shoulder or tell her how they feel about the patient's death is often the most positive action a nurse can take.

Whatever the nurse may say at such a time will often be remembered for years afterwards, and not always by the patient's next of kin, who may be too numbed to concentrate, but by others of the family who are with them. Positive, kindly statements are most helpful, especially if she can honestly reassure the bereaved that death was painless and dignified for the patient.

Not all cultural groups feel the social pressure to contain their grief and freely express it. This can be disturbing to those who have been caring for the patient and his family, perhaps especially because they are more accustomed to families trying to hide their feelings and tears. Families from some countries tend to gather around the bed at the time of a patient's death. They will cry and sob and some may even scream loudly. They may fling themselves at the body, covering it with kisses and tears. This presents little problem in the patient's own home but in a busy hospital ward (especially if it is Nightingale in design) it will undoubtedly disturb and shock other patients and their families, and some members of staff. In such cases it will help everyone if the patient can be nursed in a side room.

In many far eastern countries bereavement is contained within the family because of the strength of the extended family. With the Chinese, for example, although initially one may find that they appear to giggle at quite inopportune moments this is to save them from loss of face, and in the privacy of the family circle they will express their real feelings. In most tightly knit communities throughout the world support for the bereaved appears to be stronger. In such cases the nurse can be more sure that the bereaved will be looked after adequately.

But if the bereaved person is alone, the nurse needs to give additional support. If possible the bereaved person should not be left completely alone, especially if he or she then has to return to an empty house or hotel room. Bereavement is a lonely experience at the best of times, but if the person is in another country and in an alien culture, it can not only be lonely but frightening. The bereaved may not speak the same language as the host country. They face an unknown health care system and what often seems a formidable amount of bureaucracy. Here the nurse, doctor, minister of religion and hospital administrative staff can all be of help.

First, it is important to realize that, however long someone has lived in a country, he or she will not necessarily fully understand its institutions, traditions and its laws. A member of the indigenous population, whether immigrant or tourist, may still be totally lost when a loved one dies, a feeling further accentuated if the death was sudden.

It is helpful to explain the formalities concerning the necessity for a death certificate, a special certificate for cremation if requested, and the circumstances in which a coroner's post-mortem examination is required — if the death is one that must be reported to the coroner. The next of kin should be shown how to go about registering the death and how to deal with the patient's affairs, such as probate.

If the patient was resident in another country and only temporarily on a visit, the assistance of his country's embassy or consulate should be sought. This is particularly important if the deceased's body is to be returned to his own country for burial, as there are considerable formalities surrounding the repatriation of a body. In addition to those already mentioned, there are also Home Office regulations, health, airline and other regulations in the patient's own country.

There is also a variety of charges to pay within the United Kingdom when a body crosses parish and county boundaries. Funeral directors are familiar with these problems and most will take on the task of completing all the required formalities helped by the relevant embassy or authority, if requested to do so by the family.

Many outside agencies can be called in to help with the support and comfort of the bereaved, including a minister of the appropriate religion and denomination, the Red Cross, the Women's Royal Voluntary Service, and so on, depending on the person's particular need. The medical social worker should be consulted, if the death occurs in hospital, and the social services department if within the community, so that the most appropriate advice and help can be given.

Some countries have a tradition of a long period of mourning, as in the Mediterranean countries. Once a woman goes into mourning she wears black, and for some women this can mean that they will continue to wear it for the rest of their lives.

Birth

BEFORE BIRTH

In some countries antenatal care is not as carefully monitored as it is here and many women may not attend regular antenatal clinics. Some Asian, Chinese and Middle Eastern women refuse to undergo an antenatal vaginal examination even by a female midwife or obstetrician, and almost certainly refuse to be examined or even observed by males.

Before the birth of a Chinese baby the maternal grandmother visits her daughter with gifts of food, usually eggs, chicken and soup.

DURING BIRTH

When giving birth, many women prefer the lateral position. Among Asian, African, West Indian and Middle Eastern women the dorsal position is usually preferred. Some, however, adopt a squatting position. The lateral and dorsal positions can usually be accommodated without a problem, but modern British midwifery practice is not often geared to the squatting position! If possible this should be sorted out in advance, during antenatal classes, between the midwife, doctor and patient. The essential factor is the safe delivery of the infant without harming the mother; if this can be achieved in a way that also meets the patient's wishes then so much the better, but the baby's safety is the prime objective.

AFTER BIRTH

There are many different attitudes to birth. In most countries families look forward to having at least one son. In Asia, there is a distinctive preference for sons. In the Chinese tradition it is implicit to refer to the birth of a boy as a 'great joy' and of a girl as 'small joy'. The desire to have a son in the family often creates large families.

Among the various religions and cultures are different traditions surrounding the baby and the mother after the child's birth. In most countries the mother and baby are visited by the baby's father and both sets of grandparents, who often bring flowers for the mother and a gift for the baby. Among the Asian community there are other customs. Within a few days of the birth the family of both sets of parents visit the mother and baby. Hindus may wish to pray with the mother and place symbolic markings on the mother and child, or they may wish to bring food and share it with the mother. Sikhs celebrate in a similar way but they like to bring sweets and to distribute them, particularly if the baby is a boy. When a baby is born to a Muslim family, a member of the family must recite a very short prayer in the baby's ear.

Most Asians believe that a mother must rest for 40 days after the birth. This is because they believe that the mother is very susceptible to illness and injury at this time. They may be very distressed to find that, in western midwifery practice, the mother normally gets up and takes a bath within the first two days after delivery. The visiting relatives may need to be persuaded to leave gifts of clothing by the bedside because many will wish to follow the tradition of trying them on the baby straight away. The mother may also be very distressed if her baby is removed from her bedside, so the baby should remain with her if possible.

Many West Indian mothers ask for a copy of the Holy Bible to be placed in the baby's cot as soon as possible after birth.

The Chinese celebrate by bringing in presents of clothing, such as a bonnet and shoes for the baby, usually brought by the baby's maternal grandmother. According to tradition the baby is not washed for the first three days after birth, and then after a month his head is shaved. The father of the baby visits his near relatives to announce the birth and takes them presents of red eggs.

Naming of the baby follows different customs too. Occasionally the choice of name is not a matter for the parents, as is the custom in Europe and the United States, but, for many Asians is the choice of the father's sister or elder relatives. Sikhs often choose the name from the *Adi-Granth*, and Muslims from the Koran. Among Roman Catholics all over the world there is a tradition that the child should be given the name of one of the saints.

Feeding can also create misunderstandings. In some areas it has already been found that Hindu, and occasionally Sikh mothers, who do not speak English very well, have not grasped the purpose of dried milk. On being given Cow and Gate they have misunderstood the cow symbol, and believing it to have come from a dead cow (a sacred animal to the Hindus) have refused to give it to their babies (see also page 12).

Children

In some cultures, it is especially important to have a son, and some people may have a large family simply because they keep trying for a son without success. Among Asians, Arabs and Africans a totally different attitude towards girls from that of western society may be found; among these groups, girls are often considered to be inferior to boys. With parents who have come directly to the United Kingdom from Pakistan, Bangladesh and India, if economies have to be made, they are made over clothing for the girls rather than the boys. In some Asian countries it is a harsh fact of life that there is considerable poverty and lack of food, so if a choice has to be made on which mouths to feed, a girl child may be abandoned or neglected in order to save a boy.

Members of primary care teams and hospital personnel should be ready to give advice about the social services available to help such families, so that they are not forced to contemplate drastic choices of this kind.

Climate

Climate plays an important part in the culture of a country; it affects the diet, the form of housing, the economy, the type of clothing and various other aspects of daily life. A patient who has flown in from a very hot climate to a very cold one, and vice versa, needs time to grow accustomed to the local temperature and its consequences. Patients who normally live in very hot climates often feel very cold even during a good British summer! Many appreciate the offer of extra blankets, but some may have difficulty in sleeping because they are unaccustomed to the weight. Conversely, those going from cold to hot climates often miss the weight of the blankets.

It is also wise to check that a patient coming from a different climate is appropriately dressed when he leaves the hospital; it will not help complete recovery if he has to undertake a long journey inappropriately dressed for the climate. If the patient has no next of kin or relatives with him to provide such a change of clothes, the advice of the medical social worker (or in the community, the social services department) should be sought.

Clothing

Most patients wear western clothes. Some, however, wear their national dress. These clothes may have a social or religious significance but in many cases national dress is worn because the patient likes it, feels comfortable in it and is proud of it. (It is inappropriate to include here the national dress of countries within the United Kingdom.)

Many Chinese women like to wear the *cheongsam* (see Figure 1), a tight-fitting silk dress with a high mandarin collar and side slit. The Chinese usually wear something around their necks because they do not like them exposed; yet they may be quite unconcerned at the effects caused by their slit skirts, which may sometimes expose long expanses of thigh and be very tight-fitting!

Pakistani women wear a costume that consists of trousers which are tapered to fit the calf and ankle, and a shirt top, known as a *salwar-kameez* (see Figure 1). Like most Muslim women they must keep their bodies completely covered. Muslim women from Iran, Iraq, Saudi Arabia, the Gulf States and other parts of the Middle East wear *chador* which is a long black dress or skirt and blouse, a black veil and a hard shiny face mask (see Figure 1). Indian women frequently prefer to wear a *sari*.

When considering the cultural differences in clothing one must also think of attitudes to modesty. Many female patients from Muslim countries are extremely modest. They are accustomed to being clothed from head to foot all the time, and the prospect of being expected to be seen in public with short clothes on is abhorrent to them. Nurses must ensure that their patients' ideas of modesty are respected if they are to win their confidence and not allow them to become overanxious. As with any patient the nurse must ensure that undressing takes place in private behind closed doors or curtains. Most Muslim women refuse to undress in front of a male nurse and would prefer to undress alone or in front of a female nurse.

Even when dressed in a gown or nightdress the patient may still be embarrassed because her legs are bare, and she may refuse to get out of bed because they are not covered. If an intravenous infusion or a fractured arm makes it difficult to cover the arm with a sleeve, some other means of covering should be found.

Consent to treatment

In the United Kingdom, it is legally required for the patient to sign a form giving his consent for the medical staff to carry out a particular operation or examination. Before the operation can take place (other than in exceptionally urgent circumstances) the patient, and on occasions his next of kin, have to sign the consent form after the doctor has explained the procedure to him.

Figure 1 (a) *Cheongsam*; (b) *salwar-kameez*;
(c) *chador*; (d) orthodox jewish dress; (e) Sikh dress

Ward staff may find that women from the Far East or Middle East are reluctant to sign the form. This does not necessarily mean that the patient is refusing to give her consent, but rather that she is not used to the idea of being asked to sign such a form because in her own country it would normally be signed by a male next of kin, such as husband, father or brother. To overcome both legal and cultural difficulties, it is easier if both the patient and the male next of kin sign the consent form.

Patients from parts of mainland Europe may also be puzzled by such a form. For example, in Belgium, although the doctor requires the patient's *verbal* consent to operate, the latter's consent is implied in his admission to hospital.

If the patient does not speak English, the consent form should be translated to ensure that the patient has fully understood it before signing.

Contraception

Apart from the diverse religious attitudes to contraception, there are also a number of varying cultural attitudes, which may include not only whether it is right or wrong to practise contraception but may also question the methods used. Some individuals may agree to contraception but find some methods abhorrent. For example, in many parts of the world coitus interruptus, the rhythm method, the sheath and the cap are acceptable but the contraceptive pill, the intrauterine device (IUD) and sterilization are not. The reasons are diverse, and can be religious, emotional or superstitious. The following are a few that have been encountered:

1. The pill prevents the rebirth of a soul.
2. The coil worms its way into the baby and poisons it.
3. The pill affects the laws of nature and can damage all future generations genetically.
4. The coil is a form of early abortion. In fact many believe that this form of contraception amounts to murder by stealth because they firmly believe that the life of the individual begins at the moment of conception, so that while methods which prevent the ovum and spermatozoa meeting are acceptable, those which affect the fertilized ovum are totally unacceptable.

Vasectomy and sterilization are offensive to many because they believe that virility and fertility are linked and therefore of vital importance. In family planning clinics, care is taken to explain that one can be sterilized without losing any of one's sexuality or virility. Most often this decision is one of family, social and economics, but sometimes it is because it is dangerous for a woman to run the risk of becoming pregnant again. The question of contraception is cross-cultural and is not specific to any one culture.

Death

Death is the one absolute certainty in everyone's lives! In many societies this fact is accepted and not hidden in any way. In parts of the United Kingdom it is incorporated into the daily life of a village or town, and in some areas the body of the deceased remains in the patient's home until the burial or cremation. The coffin is placed in the sitting room or bedroom and all the family, friends and neighbours are expected to pay their last respects to the deceased in his home. Blinds or curtains are drawn in the street where the deceased lived as a mark of respect.

In other parts of the United Kingdom, death is taboo. People hide from the reality of it and, after death, the body is disposed of quickly and quietly without much ceremony. For instance, some families do not even wish to be with the patient when he dies nor to see his body after death. The body is hurriedly removed by undertakers and not seen again until the day of the funeral when it is enclosed in a wooden coffin. Some families do not even attend the funeral or cremation.

Lying in state in the United Kingdom, whether for a monarch or a loved and respected statesman, takes the form of the body being placed in a coffin which is then closed and draped with the Union Jack. By contrast, in the Roman Catholic Church, the body of the Pope lies in state so that those paying their last respects can see the person they loved and respected. This is also a tradition in Russia, and is perhaps the reason for the long queues of the devout and the curious who file past the embalmed body of Lenin in his mausoleum in Moscow's Red Square.

Nurses should not be surprised if a British family leaves very soon after the death and does not wish to see the body again. Nor should she be surprised if someone from the Middle East or the Far East wishes to stay with the body, invites all the family and friends to come and then asks to take the body home. Both these families can be accommodated. The first family poses no administrative problems. The second creates some problems, but they are not too difficult to overcome. First, as the patient's approaching death becomes obvious, he should be allowed the privacy of a side ward or a quiet part of the ward where he can die peacefully surrounded by his family, and without making the other patients anxious. After death, the immediate family should be allowed to be alone with the deceased before the last offices are performed. When the body has been laid out, the relatives should be allowed to see the body again if they wish.

If further members of the family or friends come to the hospital, the nurse can suggest that either they see the body in the hospital's mortuary chapel, where it can lie in more peaceful surroundings, or when it has been taken to his home or to the undertaker's.

For some, a death in the family is a cause for celebration as in the traditional Irish wake, a party to which the family and friends are invited to celebrate the deceased's life and achievements. The coffin is placed in the corner of the room. It is an occasion when everyone is happy that suffering is at an end for the deceased and he can now find peace in heaven.

BURIAL AND CREMATION

In some cultures, disposal of the body differs from British custom. For example, in Muslim countries burial but not cremation is acceptable and it should be carried out in the way described in the section on Islam (page 75). In Hindu India and other oriental countries, however, cremation is preferred. Newcomers to the United Kingdom should be advised about the customary form of burial and cremation in this country so they do not find themselves trying to conduct a form of burial or cremation which would be normal in their native land but totally unacceptable in the United Kingdom. Such lack of knowledge led to one incident to the author's knowledge, of an Asian family trying to cremate the grandfather on an elaborate funeral pyre in a suburban garden (*see also* Bereavement).

Diet

Climate, a country's economic situation and the ability to import and grow foods, are important factors in the diet and provision of food; the size of the population in relation to resources should also be borne in mind. Therefore, a different diet can be found among the Asian and Far Eastern peoples from that in North and South America, Africa and Europe. In addition to the ability to grow and import food, the availability of transport and of food storage must be considered. In some countries — for instance, Africa, Asia and South America — transport systems are only just developing, whereas in North America and Europe they are highly developed so the transport of food is quicker and easier. The way food can be stored is also dependent on the resources available. If electricity is available, refrigerators and deep freezers help food suppliers and consumers to store food. Where electricity is not available, the number of items and the type of food that can be stored is reduced and the diet in that country or region is adversely affected. For example, in some areas fruits are dried in order to preserve them and meat is marinated or curried. Meat is in short supply in India and China but rice, which grows in abundance, can be used to provide a substantial meal.

Many people from rural communities throughout the world shudder at the thought of frozen food, battery hens and their eggs, fish fingers and dehydrated food. They not only rebel against the way these foods are produced and presented, but claim that they can taste the difference.

Not only religion but tradition and folklore can also affect diet. In Britain our traditional foods are: breakfast of cereal, eggs, sausage and tomatoes followed by toast, marmalade and tea, or the Scottish version which includes porridge; roast beef, and Yorkshire pudding, roast potatoes and cabbage or some other vegetable for Sunday lunch; and the traditional Christmas dinner with roast turkey and plum pudding. All countries, whether European, Asian, African or American, have their traditional foods and dishes: wiener schnitzel in Austria; sauerkraut in Germany; ratatouille and french bread in France; cous-cous in North Africa; curry in India; mixtures of sweet and sour flavours in Chinese cookery; bortsch in Russia; and pumpkin pie in the United States.

This means that when a patient comes from another region or country into one of our hospitals, he may lose his appetite not only because of his illness but because of the difference in diet. This also applies to drinking water, even among Europeans, many of whom would be horrified to find a jug of tap water on their lockers! They may insist on buying bottled water. This poses no real problem except that the nurses and medical staff concerned with the care of the patient must bear in mind that the electrolyte content of some of these bottled waters is different, and some are high in sodium chloride. For the majority of patients this presents no problem but it could affect the care of a patient on a strict salt-free diet, or one with diabetes insipidus.

The patient may also find the time and way of eating our various meals to be equally strange. If, for example, he has come straight from the other side of the globe he may have jet lag and his biological cycle may be as disturbed as that of a night nurse! He may not be familiar with the times at which the British eat their meals; for instance, in some countries the main meal is eaten at lunch while in others it is late in the evening. In most countries the timing of meals is determined by both social factors and climate.

There are many variations on this in Britain alone. In some parts of Britain it is normal to have a meal at 5 or 6 pm; this is known as high tea and consists of hot or cold meat or fish, with or without vegetables, followed by bread, scones, conserves of some kind, either jam or honey, cake and tea. Others prefer a dinner at about 7.30 or 8 pm which includes an entrée, main course and dessert followed by coffee.

The way a meal is served and eaten also varies within cultural groups. A Chinese or Japanese patient may be used to eating out of bowls using chopsticks; but the majority of Chinese and Japanese likely to be nursed in the United Kingdom are familiar with the British way of eating. There are, however, other more subtle differences especially on the mainland of Europe. In France, for example, meat and vegetables are seldom served together; one is served after the other and a French person may find a mixture on the plate unappetizing. It may also take some patients a little while to become accustomed to the combinations of 'meat and two veg' that they find on a British plate.

Folklore can also be used to aid recovery — for example, spinach gives one strong muscles, carrots makes one see in the dark, etc. Both these foods have nutrients and there is some element of truth in their claims; spinach contains iron and carrots contain vitamins essential for good eyesight.

'HOT AND COLD' FOODS

A complex tradition surrounds Indian thinking about the contents of foodstuffs. Indians believe that foods are in themselves hot or cold, but this does not refer to the *temperature* of the food — hot does not mean straight out of the oven, nor cold out of the refrigerator. According to Storer's (1977) work on 'hot' and 'cold' food beliefs, 'hot' and 'cold' are described as follows.

> Most foods with a pungent, acidic or salty taste were considered 'hot', and foods with a sweet, astringent or bitter taste were 'cold'. The 'hot' foods were said to produce giddiness, thirst, bodily exhaustion or fatigue, sweating, inflammatory reactions and accelerated chemical reactions on digestion; 'cold' foods were said to cause cheerfulness and pleasure of mind, to sustain life and to impart strength, sturdiness and steadiness to the body.

The same foodstuff may be 'hot' in one part of India and 'cold' in another thereby making it difficult to give really practical advice to non-Hindus. In these circumstances, if there are no Indians among the staff of the hospital, it may be helpful to contact the nearest community relations council for advice.

VEGETARIANS

Many patients are vegetarians for reasons other than religious ones. It may be that they are allergic to meat or fish, or because they find the killing of animals abhorrent. It may also be because they do not like the taste of meat or fish. There are some vegetarians who will not eat anything at all from an animal, including eggs, milk, fish roe, jelly, cooking fat, cheese and butter. Such patients may wish to supply their own particular favourite forms of non-animal protein so that their diet is not too lacking in vegetable protein.

EATING HABITS

Everyone has their own habits which reflect personality, social background, education and national characteristics. These are easy to accommodate within the home but they may need to be modified slightly outside. When a patient comes into hospital he has many adjustments to make and one of them is to his personal routine and habits, apart from conforming to hospital meals and mealtimes.

He is also expected to mix with people he has never met before, often to sleep in the same room and eat his food with them. He may be shepherded into a communal dining room as soon as he is on his feet. It is remarkable that patients cope with all these changes as well as they do. Nurses should be sensitive to the problems of communal eating in hospital, for some patients lose their appetite because they are repelled by someone sitting at the table beside them with a urinary drainage bag, or with a suppurating wound — or perhaps they are sensitive about their own purulent wound or a colostomy bag. Others are embarrassed and offended by those who have a productive cough, or those who find eating difficult because they are paralysed — the latter probably feel shy and embarrassed too. The nurse acts as a catalyst in these situations, and by a sensitive understanding of the problem can help people to overcome a difficulty which they often cannot resolve themselves. Sometimes it is better to encourage a patient to eat by his bedside so that others can eat their meals feeling more at ease.

Some patients are embarrassed because they come from a different social group from others at the table and they find difficulty in making conversation. Fortunately, this is usually a temporary difficulty, and often leads to people talking about their operations over lunch (which can also be unappetizing!) merely because it is something they all have in common.

Finally, when considering patients' social background it should be remembered that not all the poor and undernourished come from social classes 4 and 5. Many are from the elderly of all social classes. Just because a frail elderly patient enters the hospital proud and articulate with the appearance of a wealthy upper middle class existence does not mean that all is as it seems. Perhaps, for example, after a few hearty meals a female patient begins to feel ill and has a high blood urea; on close questioning it may be discovered that she rarely eats protein because she can no longer afford it, and because she is not used to preparing her own meals but cannot now afford a cook or housekeeper.

Similarly the poor person who has not used his social security payments to buy nutritious food may find coming into hospital for investigations paradise because of the meals, but after a sudden change in diet he too may feel unwell (see also section on social class, page 43).

Drugs

Some patients find the taking of any kind of drug unpleasant, and are often the kind of people who would rather suffer pain than take an analgesic. In some countries (particularly Arab), if the drugs are not given by injection, they are not thought to be efficacious. Some Europeans prefer to have their drugs by suppository. This is not impossible in the United Kingdom, but the pharmacy may need time to order them. Many patients bring their drugs with them; here it is important to find the approved name of the drug, as many of the drug companies market the same drug in different countries under different proprietary names. The nearest poisons centre will give the contents of the drug.

Occasionally patients come into hospital after having smoked cannabis or marijuana. Some people feel that it helps them to meditate and relax and they equate it with alcohol, despite the fact that it is still against the law. It is easy to be confident when in a crowd but, when brought into hospital under the effects of the drug, not all marijuana smokers are proud and boastful. But whereas taking drugs is often a sign of rebellion or inadequacy among the young of the indigenous population, in the East the drug is cultivated legally, and patients may genuinely not be aware that the drug is illegal in the United Kingdom. Such cases are, however, rare.

Education

It is important to have some idea of a patient's educational background. This can be determined by a number of factors apart from the patient's occupation, which is becoming a less accurate rule of thumb as opportunities for education diversify, for example, evening classes and the Open University. On the other hand, many university graduates are in manual jobs.

Establishing the patient's educational level gives the doctor, nurse and others the clues to the kind of information he needs and in what kind of language it must be given. If the patient is a doctor or biology teacher his concept of his body may be vastly different from that of an artist or a manual worker who has studied no biology but has an interest in physical fitness and sport. Different imagery and terminology may be needed in each case to explain exactly what is wrong with the patient and what is going to be done to and for him. Language is discussed in a section of its own (page 37), but in this context it is as well to remember that people who are intelligent and well-informed in their own language may tend to be treated as fools simply because they cannot express themselves succinctly, fluently or quickly in another.

The ability to read and write is another factor. Among the British population there are still some who cannot read or write. They often camouflage this problem very well and it may only come to light if the patient has to read or write something in hospital, when he may have to ask the nurse to tell him what is written on the consent form or bottle of tablets. There are special adult reading units throughout the country, and the medical social worker or health visitor may be able to assist the non-reader in his long-term needs. This also presents itself in some patients from overseas who speak English but cannot read or write it.

The elderly

There are many different cultural attitudes towards the elderly, varying from a loving and dutiful respect to complete disregard. Respect and love may be felt for an individual because of his own particular qualities. Or they can arise out of a sense of duty towards a respected elderly member of the family — feelings which may or may not be extended to elderly persons outside the family.

Cultural differences often originate in the concept of duty and the way this duty is manifested in practical terms. In Britain many elderly people are supported in some way by their families both in emotional and financial terms. But once they become totally dependent physically, mentally and socially they are more likely to become the responsibility of the State or of some outside body, because the extended family and closeknit communities are diminishing. More and more married women are going out to work, and therefore many elderly people live in houses or flats in what have become dormitory villages.

Among the Chinese, perhaps due to the influence of centuries of Confucianism, there is a marked sense of duty towards the elderly which is helped by the extended family. This duty is shared by the family because they regard it as the correct thing to do, and it is maintained even if the elderly person is not particularly well-loved. Sadly, this may change among subsequent generations of Chinese people in Britain because of the pressures of our society.

The extended family can also give effective support even though the members of the family are scattered throughout the world. For example, thousands of people in the United Kingdom are working here in order to send a percentage of their salary back to their parents or grandparents in their native land.

There are, however, some cultures where, mainly for economic reasons, the elderly are set aside and neglected because, for example, there is not enough food to go round.

Etiquette

In the United Kingdom it is polite for a stranger to be called Mr, Mrs or Miss followed by the surname. Later when the relationship develops into a friendship the person's Christian name is used. In some countries this does not happen at all. In Japan, for example, the forename is used only between close family and very close friends of long standing. The most common form of address in Japan is to give a man's surname followed by the term 'san'). Mr Jones, therefore, would be addressed as Jones-san.

In Europe, a definite distinction is made between young and older women. For example, in French-speaking countries it is usual to address a man as *'monsieur'*, women under about the age of 25 as *'mademoiselle'*, unless she is married when she is addressed as *'madame'*. Any unmarried woman over the age of about 25 to 30 should also be addressed as *'madame'*. The same principles apply in Germany and Holland.

It is customary in Britain for men to open doors for women to enter or leave a room in front of them. In Asia, it is the opposite — a man walks ahead of a woman or child; this is considered polite because the man is offering the woman or his children his protection.

In some countries it is the custom to shake hands when you first meet someone. In others you shake hands every time you meet or leave someone. In some European countries it is the custom for men and women to greet their family and friends with a kiss on both cheeks.

Gestures

Every country has its rude gestures! The problem is that what is a rude gesture to some is not to others, and vice versa! But aside from rude gestures, some countries have developed quite a complex language of gestures which may be used to emphasize speech or may, on occasions, be used instead of it.

Face

The oriental idea of face relates to a personal concept of honour and can strongly influence attitudes to pain. Anyone who has nursed a Gurkha soldier will have been impressed by his high tolerance for pain and his cheerful acceptance of it. Usually it must be explained to him that the administration of analgesia is a routine treatment in his case and is no reflection on his soldierly honour (motto: 'It is better to die than to live a coward') nor on his ability to endure pain. Face is also important for Chinese and Japanese patients who tend to have a high tolerance for pain and great care must be taken, with patients of this type, to monitor them for symptoms of pain, since they themselves seldom draw attention to it. A Gurkha may deny that he feels any pain at all — even if he is in agony. And if, *in extremis*, he lets the cat out of the bag, this is usually accompanied by an apology! Gurkhas, Chinese and Japanese often smile, laugh or giggle when in pain or under stress of any kind. This symptom should be looked for if it occurs when there is no apparent source of humour.

But face can have other, less ennobling, manifestations. It is roughly synonymous with 'pride', but much more complicated and important, and forms a complex matrix with custom, religion and culture. Aspects of it are dealt with in other relevant sections. In Eastern and oriental societies it is generally more important for men than for women, and often governs the relationship between them. In dealing with patients it can be very difficult and tiresome since, for example, it is loss of face for many Muslims to be told what to do by a woman. It thus becomes a point of honour for them to do exactly the opposite of what the nurse has told them. This can easily be confused with problems of language and education, and it can also have serious repercussions when dealing with some Eastern doctors.

To take an interesting example from the author's experience: for a midnight case of respiratory arrest the senior house officer on duty, who was from the Middle East, was called simultaneously with the anaesthetist. The house officer, who lived in the hospital flats and was within three minutes of the ward, had been warned of this possible emergency during the night, knew that the anaesthetist was about to start another case, and had frequently intubated patients before. The anaesthetist, who lived a little further away, was already dealing with the other case and could not leave immediately, but still got to the ward before the house officer — unshaven, hair awry, and wearing a mixture of jeans and pyjamas! He was too late to do anything for the patient, who, despite attempts at resuscitation and external cardiac massage, had gone into cardiac arrest and died. The senior house officer then arrived, immaculately dressed, asking what he could do to help. The furious night sister replied coldly that, since he had taken 25 minutes to move a short distance, he could now only sign the death certificate. The anaesthetist was equally enraged when the houseman said that he could not appear on the ward in front of nurses (the important point to him!) without first having a bath, a shave and then dressing immaculately, even down to his gold cufflinks. The point of all this is that, to him, the question of face, *vis-à-vis* the nurses, was of much greater consequence than the possible death of a patient. Nor did his viewpoint change as a result of this incident and, while this sort of conflict cannot be tolerated on the wards, it must be allowed for, anticipated and evaded; it can also be modified or eradicated by firm handling and training (*see also* Fear; Pain; Indifference to death).

Family and friends

To patients throughout the world family and friends are always important. In some countries, however, the family is a particularly closeknit entity, remaining in close contact and supporting each other when times are hard, such as during illness. This is particularly so in Japan and China and other parts of the Far East, and nurses may find that these patients usually have considerable support from their families, and if they are totally cut off from them will feel such a loss very keenly indeed.

Some patients who come from first-generation immigrant families have difficulty in reconciling some of the attitudes found in hospital with those of their family. First-generation families are those in which the parents were born and educated overseas, and the children were born and educated in the United Kingdom. Some examples of the conflict can best be illustrated by the introduction of mixed sex wards where a young man and woman can find themselves wandering about in their nightclothes and dressing gowns, and may even eat at the same table dressed this way.

Imagine, for instance, that the strict Muslim parents of a young girl come to visit her in hospital and find her sitting chatting to a young man both dressed in their nightclothes. The young girl has been educated in a modern comprehensive school, and thinks little of it except for the nagging feeling that her parents will create a fuss. In fact, to her parents such a situation is shameful and outrageous. A frank discussion between the girl and her parents may help to produce a compromise but it is better to ensure that she has a place in the ward far from the men and to which she can retire before visiting hours to minimize the anxiety of her parents.

For some people who live in very mobile societies where families are often considerable distances apart, friends can play a more important role than the family. The law insists on permission for operations being given by the next of kin, if the patient cannot give it himself. In some cases the next of kin has had no contact with the patient for several years and may not be aware of his current views. If the patient has close friends who know his wishes their views should also be considered (*see also* Marriage).

Fear

While fear can be related to pain, the two are not synonymous. People with eastern backgrounds can have a casual attitude towards life which strongly colours their reactions to fear, sickness and death. While as patients they may be highly sensitive to their surroundings and to some ethical aspects of their treatment, nursing care and personal hygiene they may, on the other hand, be relatively indifferent to death on the ward or to the sight of injury or blood. But, paradoxically, they may be terrified at the sight or sound of modern equipment that can save their lives! They may show little sign of fear with strong reactions to pain, but not often vice versa. As stated above 'face' may forbid Gurkha, Chinese and Japanese patients, especially, from showing signs of either fear or pain (*see* Face; Indifference to death).

Handicap

Attitudes to handicap vary, and depend on the form of handicap and the society in which the handicapped person has lived and worked. In some countries a handicapped person is regarded as an unacceptable burden. So the patient may not always be filled with joy and gratitude at the thought of repatriation because he may fear total rejection by his family, friends and fellow countrymen.

Health care systems

The National Health Service is unique. There are many other state health services but they differ in some respect from that in the United Kingdom. For example, there is the friendly society insurance scheme which prevails in Europe, the private health care and insurance schemes in the United States. In developing countries, with an incomplete or embryo state health service, there is the dependence on Church missions and United Nations charitable organizations.

All these systems have considerable advantages and disadvantages. It is perhaps useful to say that some of the orientation difficulties faced by patients from abroad are caused by their lack of knowledge and understanding of how the National Health Service works. To begin with, many try to shop around for the best doctor without realizing that National Health Service patients have a limited choice and must be referred by a general practitioner. Some potential patients have been known to head for Harley Street only to find that consultations there are private and not part of the National Health Service.

On the mainland of Europe and in the United States prospective patients look for a specialist rather than going to a general practitioner. In France if one has a headache, one consults either a neurologist or a general practitioner – the choice is an open one; similarly for chest pain one may go to a cardiologist, general practitioner, chest physician or general surgeon. Most people from these countries do not realize that emergency treatment under the National Health Service is free to all (apart from those who deliberately abuse this humanitarian service). For those who have paid income tax and national health insurance, all treatment is free at the point of delivery with a few exceptions such as prescription charges, dental care and spectacles, where charges are made in some cases. Some patients may be anxious about taking drugs, or about when they leave the hospital, fearing that if they do not leave before a certain time they will have to pay an extra day's board. This is because in some other countries of Europe and in America the patient receives a bill at the end of his stay; although his insurance may pay most of the bill, he may still have to pay as much as 20 to 30 per cent of it himself.

Some Asian and African patients may bring a very large sum of money to the hospital as payment in advance rather than a fee for services rendered; it may be difficult to convince patients that they will still receive good care without paying the doctor in advance! The local community relations council should be contacted if there is no-one in the hospital who can explain this properly.

Not all health care systems have such a mixture of races and cultures in their hospitals. In South Africa, for instance, hospital treatment for blacks and cape coloureds is separate from that for whites. On coming to the United Kingdom, members of all three racial groups may find it hard at first to adjust to a multiracial health care system.

Hygiene

Many European, Asian and Arab patients prefer showers to baths, and object to sitting in a bath because they regard it as sitting in dirty water. Asian women, in particular, are very reluctant to take a bath or shower if a nurse is with them because they object to being seen naked by others, especially males.

Many old people from remote rural parts of Britain and abroad are terrified by showers and baths because they are unused to them. They may not even have hot and cold running water, mains sewerage, central heating, gas or electricity. These old people are used to washing themselves thoroughly, and usually adequately, by undressing a part of the body, washing and drying it and replacing the clothes there. In this way they wash each part in turn and remain warm. Changing clothes this way is much more difficult, but most patients have a system of their own!

Muslims, Jews and some other religious groups have their own particular religious ablutions (see Figure 4, pages 76 and 77). Some Arabic patients, who are nearly all Muslims, also reserve one hand for food-handling and the other for cleaning the anal area after defaecation. If either hand is paralysed, injured or otherwise unfit for use the nurse will need to assist the patient with eating or cleaning, or find some other ingenious and acceptable solution.

Illness

In most western countries illness is taken as being very unfortunate, and for which all help and support must be offered. It is not regarded as something of which to be ashamed. But, even today there are strong prejudices against psychiatric illness, and the patient often has to carry the stigma of having had such an illness as well as coping with the illness itself. In some countries in parts of Africa and Asia there is an unfortunate tendency to regard a sick or handicapped person as an unwanted burden, and the patient may be rejected by his family, friends and even by society itself.

Some countries have folk traditions and superstitions which may affect the patient's attitude to treatment and some aspects of care. For example, in some African states, and sometimes among Polynesians and aborigines, psychotic illness is regarded with terror as they believe that such a patient is possessed by the devil or evil spirits. While it is rare to find Africans, Polynesians and aborigines holding these views in British hospitals you may find that anyone from those countries studying and living in Britain may have problems when returning to his own country following such a mental illness (*see also* Handicap).

Indifference to death

It is not only a patient's indifference to death that can be relevant but some eastern doctors — even otherwise good ones — can also be indifferent to it. It can be traumatic for doctors and nurses, who have been helping a patient for whom there is still hope in a valiant struggle for life, who telephone a senior registrar during the night — only to be told that it is hardly worth proceeding further since the case is terminal, the patient over 40 and has had a good life!

There may come a point when both clinical judgement and humanity can combine after appropriate consultation and much agonizing, into an ethical decision 'neither to kill, nor to strive officiously to keep alive' against the interests and wishes of the patient and his family. But a casual and extreme attitude of this kind, applied where there is still a hope of recovery and of a useful life thereafter, in a patient who is the centre of a loving family and with dependent children, is profoundly shocking. The fact that it is not intended to be cruel but arises from a different cultural attitude to age and death is no compensation. Obviously this kind of problem results in doctors and senior nurses appealing to consultants over the heads of their superiors, and creates serious friction, as indeed it should. In the case outlined above the patient walked out of hospital cured, due to the perseverance and medical instinct of a young houseman, not yet registered, and the skill and understanding of a consultant surgeon (*see also* Death; Face; Fear; Shock).

Language

If a patient cannot speak, read or write his own language, then difficulties will arise. He may not be able to speak because he is deaf or dumb or both. He may not be able to read and write because he has not yet learnt to, for a number of reasons: he may be too young; or he may be physically or mentally handicapped — for instance, dyslexic, blind, aphasic or paralysed.

Imagine if, in addition to having one or a combination of those handicaps, the patient does not understand the language or dialect of those around him — isolation, loneliness, anxiety, and misunder-standing are much more likely to occur. Dysphasic patients, for example, share a lot in common with the non-English speaking visitor to Britain. They are frequently treated as if they are completely deaf and stupid; many people shout at them and use the affected forms of speech usually reserved for children. Neither is appropriate.

Writing is less of a problem in hospital and in primary care, but reading and speaking are extremely important. The following are some of the possibilities for diminishing the effects of difficulties in reading and speaking.

REGIONAL ACCENTS AND DIALECTS

In the United Kingdom there are hundreds of different regional accents and dialects; accents can be less difficult to understand if a person speaks clearly and slowly, whereas dialects can be difficult for both staff and patient alike.

Once when working in Scotland the author asked a patient in what she considered to be plain English with a hint of London in the accent, 'How are you today?' No reply was received nor to subsequent questions, so as the author was working on a neurosurgical unit, she judged the patient to be too drowsy to answer her questions. Having reported her observations the author found that her colleagues were amazed at this disclosure. To clarify the situation she and a colleague carried out another assessment of the patient together. When the colleague asked the patient how he was in the local dialect, she received an immediate reply. The author realized that if she was to continue working in that unit she had to learn the dialect!

There are also phrases in local dialects which may mean slightly or completely different things in Oxford English, and amusing and some-times embarrassing situations may ensue if care is not taken to fully understand what is being said.

FOREIGN LANGUAGES

Some patients may not have English as a first language. For them life has additional problems because, in many cases, they cannot make themselves perfectly understood, and sometimes have to rely com-pletely on sign language. If there is someone on the staff who speaks the same language this can be invaluable to the doctor, especially when taking a history and examining the patient. Alternatively a member of the family or a friend may be bilingual and may agree to interpret for both the patient and the doctor. If neither is available, then the patient's embassy should be contacted or, if appropriate, the local community relations council. Sometimes both parties can speak a third language fluently or at least adequately; recently the author nursed a Flemish patient who could not speak French or English, so both communicated as well as could be in German!

Foreign patients who are deaf and blind or deaf and dumb and can use the manual alphabets can also communicate fairly easily if there is someone available who can not only read the signs used in the deaf/blind and deaf/dumb alphabets but can also translate the signs into English.

PLEASE AND THANK YOU

Among the many British customs which baffle the visitor is the ability to say 'thank you' when meaning 'please'. For example, many patients say 'thank you' when offered a second helping of food or another cup of tea, meaning 'thank you very much for being so kind, yes; I would like another!' rather than 'no thank you'. Foreign nurses tend to misunderstand and do not give them anything further.

There is also a tendency among some British patients to consider it impolite to accept something the first time that it is offered. So this sort of ritual may occur:

Nurse: Would you like a cup of tea, Mrs Jones?
Mrs Jones: No, thank you.
Nurse: Are you sure you wouldn't like another cup of tea?
Mrs Jones: Well, yes all right. Yes, that would be very nice.

This happens much less among the young but one can see why some foreign patients find it hard to understand why they are asked twice when they have already said 'no'!

If the patient has some or all of the language difficulties outlined above life can be made intolerable by medical and nursing terminology. Whether he comes from a different educational and social background, or whether he speaks English as a foreign language, the patient needs to be able to understand what is being asked of him in plain English. A person whose first language is not English is much more likely to give an accurate answer to 'How much do you drink each day?' than 'What is your normal daily fluid intake?'

This can be best illustrated with a true story. The author was once teaching a student nurse on the ward when an extraordinary exchange was heard coming from the other side of the screen. A young houseman's voice was saying 'Have you any problems of micturition?' There was no reply. The doctor repeated his question. Still no reply. A middle-aged, motherly nurse then came in to put something on the patient's locker, and realizing that the patient had no idea what the doctor was talking about said in a kindly Cockney voice, 'What he means, dear, is can you pee all right?' to which the doctor duly got his reply. Undaunted, the houseman then asked 'Is the pressure and flow constant and uninterrupted?', to which the nurse, coming to patient's rescue yet again, said 'What he means this time, luv, is how far can you pee, for how long and does it dribble in the middle?' The history was duly completed in this way, with the nurse interpreting for the doctor!

LANGUAGES SPOKEN BY FAR EAST PATIENTS

Asian patients speak a variety of languages and dialects, and in seeking an interpreter it is important to find one who speaks a dialect or language which is common to both parties. In India, for example, Sikhs speak Punjabi or Hindu; many Indians in Britain come from Gujarat where they speak Gujarati or Hindi. Most Indians speak Hindi. Indians and Pakistanis may be able to communicate in Hindustani; Pakistanis speak Punjabi or Urdu, and those from Bangladesh speak Bengali or Hindu.

Chinese patients can usually understand each other although there are many different dialects and languages in China. However, most of the Chinese living in the United Kingdom come from Hong Kong where the language is Cantonese or Hakka. Those from Singapore may speak one of the Chinese languages or Malay depending on the cultural group from which they come.

Marriage

In the west marriage is a matter which is decided by the individuals concerned. If two people wish to marry they can do so provided that they are of the minimum age and fulfil the other legal requirements laid down in the country in which they are to be espoused. In the United Kingdom, marriage ceremonies are usually performed in a place of worship or in the local registry office. In exceptional circumstances they may take place at the bedside of a sick person. If the patient wishes to marry, is in a sound state of mind, and from one of the denominations represented by the hospital chaplains, arrangements can be made with the appropriate hospital chaplain and the local registrar of births, marriages and deaths. If the patient is from another sect or religion, which is not represented by the hospital chaplains, then the local registrar of births, marriages and deaths should be consulted along with the appropriate minister of religion. The local registrar should also be consulted if the patient is an atheist.

In some countries, marriage is not a matter of individual choice based on mutual trust and love but an arrangement made by a family on behalf of a daughter of the family. Arranged marriages are found in the Far East, Middle East and Indian subcontinent. From a very young age a girl from such a country will be introduced to her fiancé either in person or by an exchange of photographs.

Conflict arises if one or both of the parties has been brought up and educated in the west; this conflict is usually between the desire to marry a person of their own choice, which will result in a break with the family, or the need to comply with their parents' culture and marry someone that he or she does not necessarily love and may not even know. Sometimes the anxiety of this conflict will, in itself, lead to illness (*see also* Family and friends).

Names

First, for the patient's safety, it is advisable to make sure that his names are recorded accurately. Second, for the sake of the administrators and medical staff, it is important that a standardized system of recording names is adhered to so that medical records are readily available when needed. Third, it is an obvious matter of courtesy to address the patient by his correct name.

In Christian countries each individual normally has one or more Christian names followed by a surname or family name, for example, John David Smith. In some European countries (for example, France) everyone has to carry an identity card by law. As a result a married woman may be called by both her own surname and her husband's. On coming into hospital she may offer her maiden name, because in French and Belgian hospitals it is customary for female patients to have records in their maiden name. So it is wise to ask any patient from a European country for his or her identity card (they will not be upset as they will be used to such a request). So if, for instance, Monsieur Jean Dubois marries Mademoiselle Françoise Legrand his wife may be known as Madame Dubois, Madame Legrand or Madame Dubois-Legrand!

Among the Asian community customs are different and care should be taken when asking the patient for his name. Both the nurse, admissions clerk or anyone else should be clear which is his family name (which serves as surname), which is his given or first name, and which is his middle name. Very often the three can be confused, as when asked for his full name the patient might be in the habit of quoting his first and middle name, as he is used to treating his second name as his surname (this may simply be his everyday preference). On the other hand, he might of course quote his first name and his proper surname leaving out his middle name. Therefore, it is important to get the patient to mention all three of his names, so that the surname (or family name) can be accurately recorded for administrative purposes. Women usually have only a first name and a surname or family name.

The following is a selection of common Indian, Pakistani and Bangladeshi names.

Surnames
Bengali Hindu: Banerji or Bannerji or Banerjea, Chatterji, Das Gupta, Sen Gupta, Bhattarcharya or Bhattacharjee
Gujarati Hindu: Desai, Gandhi, Naik, Patel

Hindu: Agarwal or Aggarwal, Mathur, Verma, Rajpal
Sikh and Punjabi: Gill, Grewal, Kapur or Kapoor, Maini, Sandhu and Kohli
Muslim: Sayyid, Quraishi, Akbar, Tanvir, Mirza.

First names for men
Muslim: Yusuf or Yousef, Mohammed, Igbal, Hassan, Azad, Aziz
Hindu: Prashanta, Gopal, Ramesh, Suresh, Naresh, Viresh
Sikh* and Punjabi: Rattan, Kuldip, Shivdev, Dalip, Guldip, Hardeep, Jarnail, Jaswant.

First names for women
Muslim: Farzana, Ramzani, Saira, Zaira
Hindu: Kamal, Anita, Sushila, Priya, Sushma
Sikh and Punjabi: Amrita, Sunila, Gul, Suhela, Rani.

Courtesy titles for men (taking the place of Mr)
Muslim: Haji, Maulvi, Sheikh or Shaikh, Khan or Mia
Hindus: Sri or Shri, Chaudhri or Chaudhuri, Pandit, Bhai
Punjabi or Sikh: Sardar.

Courtesy titles for women
Muslim: Begum, Bibi
Hindus: Shrimati (Mrs), Kumari (Miss)
Sikh: Sardarni.

The Chinese usually write their names with the surname first followed by the given name. For example, Mao Tse-Tung, Mao being the surname and Tse-Tung the given name (see also Etiquette, page 31).

Shock

It has been observed that some oriental, Asian and negroid people can succumb to clinical shock unexpectedly or show surprisingly strong reactions to what seems to be moderate trauma. This may be for reasons that are partly cultural, certainly psychosomatic and, in some cases, purely physiological. For example, it is now well known among anaesthetists that some negroid people have a blood trait (sickle cell trait) that makes them highly sensitive to anaesthesia, and this always requires special attention. Doctors and nurses should be aware of these factors in postoperative and trauma cases. Oriental races who react stoically to fear and pain are not necessarily immune from these phenomena. Some people from cultures which are indifferent to death, and who therefore

---

*Note Singh is the middle name of most Sikh males, with Kaur as the female equivalent. If a man wishes to use Singh as his surname, his wife should be called Mrs Singh and not Mrs Kaur unless she and her husband use Kaur as a surname.

develop a fatalistic attitude to life, do not enjoy a high degree of psychosomatic will for recovery. Physiologically, diet may also be a factor through its influence on physical resistance and on the blood. Taking the nursing history gives nurses a chance to become aware of any extreme attitudes a patient may have had towards diet. Religion can also be a general pointer.

Social class

The patient's perception of his social class can be observed in many ways. It can, however, be very deceptive because some people consider social class so important that they will exhibit great pride in being from a particular social background or in having changed to what they consider to be a more worthy class from a lower class. There can be either a pride, or a sense of shame, in being 'upper', 'middle' or 'working' class.

Many people spend a lot of time and effort trying to change from one class to another because they find the social norms and activities of one class more important or desirable than another. Often this change is stimulated because of education, occupation or marriage, but sometimes a person makes a more artificial and deliberate choice and this causes extreme sensitivity to any hint that he or she comes from a different class. Whether a nurse considers class to be important or not, she has to to recognize that it exists in most societies and it is useful to understand the indigenous class structure and its differing attitudes. It must also be remembered that the norms of the doctors and nurses are not always those of the patient, and that sometimes patients are ill at ease with the attitudes and habits of those in the hospital professions.

CASTE

Indians have a very rigid class system which is called 'caste', based on the Hindu belief in reincarnation and rebirth, and is often associated with occupation. Each individual is born into a caste. He must accept that caste, marry someone from the same caste and not eat or associate with someone from another caste. This rigid system is accepted because the Hindus believe that they will be reborn into another caste in a future incarnation.

The highest Indian castes are the priests, soldiers and skilled craftsmen (in order of importance). The priests are known as Brahmins, the soldiers Kshatryas and skilled craftsmen Vaishyas. The latter include agricultural workers, artisans and businessmen. Hindus consider these castes to have been reborn already.

After these three castes come numerous others but the majority of people come within the Shudras. This caste includes all kinds of workers who in some way help the three highest castes. The subdivisions of this caste are numerous depending on the occupation involved.

Then there are the Untouchables, workers such as cleaners, fishermen and those who work in slaughterhouses considered among Hindus to be unclean. In the lowest caste of all are the Pariahs who include those who clean the streets and toilets.

Understanding the caste system may help the staff caring for Hindu patients in hospital and in the home; it influences every facet of the Hindu's working life including the profession he follows, the system of arranged marriages and his difficulty in accepting social invitations. In the hospital this could mean that he may prefer to eat by his bedside rather than with other patients. However, many Hindus now living in the United Kingdom appear to attach less importance to caste than those visiting from the Asian subcontinent.

Superstition

Of the thousands of possible superstitious beliefs that exist, some need to be looked at with care when nursing the sick. People who are not normally superstitious often suddenly become so in hospital.

Many believe that putting red and white flowers in a vase will bring bad luck. In the United Kingdom, lilac brought into a room is regarded by many as a sign of bad luck. This is not the case in many European countries and maytime in an English ward with the arrival of continental visitors bringing lilac can make some British patients quite upset.

Being in bed number 13 can also worry many patients; in some hospitals this is overcome by calling it bed 12A which most patients find acceptable. If a large group is sitting down to eat it would be wise to see whether there are thirteen people at the table and, if someone is anxious about it, it is best to rearrange the seating a little in order to overcome the problem.

There are also many superstitions concerning treatment. Some are real superstitions, and others are old wives' tales such as the belief that taking off blankets when a patient is pyrexial will give him a cold or pneumonia.

Women

Among female patients hospital staff will find a variety of cultural differences. This may be on a small scale within the indigenous population, but there are some very important cultural differences to take into account when caring for patients from other nationalities.

There is, above all else, a major difference in the attitude towards women and their role in society. Among Muslims, in particular, a woman has a very restricted role in life — to marry, obey her husband, run her home and to rear children. Many will say that they are no different in that respect to most other women throughout the world! But in most

Muslim countries such as Pakistan, Saudi Arabia, Iraq and Iran a woman cannot make an important decision on her own. She cannot, for example, sign her consent form. Her husband (or father if she is unmarried) must sign it for her. In the United Kingdom the patient must sign her own consent form but, if this will upset the patient and her family, it is often wise to let both her and her husband sign the form.

Problems can arise if the patient wants the operation but her husband does not agree with her. In this case the patient, doctor and next of kin must discuss the problem and arrive at a decision accordingly. The doctor usually tries to influence the family towards the clinical good of the patient, but he should respect religious and cultural objections to this.

Muslim women also wear clothes which cover the whole body except the hands (the arms, ankles and neck must not be seen). In Iran and parts of Arabia this is known as *chador* (see Figure 1, page 23). Many women also wear a covering like a mask around the eyes and the nose. The mouth is usually hidden by the same cloth that covers the head, a loose fold which is often held between the teeth.

In Pakistan the *chador* is replaced by the *salwar-kameez* and a scarf which covers the head, and also the mouth and nose. Most of these women are confined to the home, as neither their religion nor culture permit them to go out to work. This means that if they go to the doctor, to the clinic or to the hospital they are often very anxious and feel lost and abandoned; they often have to fend for themselves in this way because male members of the family are at work.

Not only do these women feel it strange to be away from their homes but many of them do not speak English. They feel shy and embarrassed because the experience is new and they cannot express themselves easily. Wherever possible a member of staff of the hospital or clinic who speaks the patient's language should be found. This is ideal, but where it is not possible help can be provided by the local community relations council. The Health Education Council also publishes several health care leaflets in various Asian languages.

Women from most of the Middle East, Africa, the Indian subcontinent and the Far East will not undress in front of men. This has been mentioned elsewhere in the book in various contexts, but I wish to emphasize here the real horror that some women feel — not only those from eastern groups, but also some British women who resent being exposed in front of a group of staring men as is frequently found on hospital ward rounds. Most eastern women, and many British, American and continental women as well prefer to be cared for by female members of staff.

Some Arab and Asian women are extremely reluctant to discuss sexual matters at all. Some women needing gynaecological treatment are found on examination to have been subjected to quite brutal surgery to the external genitalia, most frequently a clitorectomy and resection of the labia, which is still performed regularly in some Arab and African states.

Sometimes young girls who have had a sexual experience since leaving their country will later ask to have their hymens made intact so that they can marry in their home country. This is very important to them because they cannot marry into a good family if they are not virgins. This presents a dilemma for the doctor because it is difficult to arrange, in a sense it is ethically fraudulent, and in reality a perforated hymen does not necessarily mean the girl has had sexual intercourse. On the other hand an imperforate hymen does not always mean that the girl is a virgin. Many Arab and African women refuse a vaginal examination for this reason.

One of the reasons for having an imperforate hymen is that, in some Arab and African states, men may still follow the tradition of brutal sexual intercourse when first married; this can cause a lot of damage to the woman's genitalia and much psychological distress. Even though there is considerable blood loss few women will call a doctor. As a result, when they become pregnant many of these women are very anaemic.

Another point to consider is that, in some countries, polygamy is tolerated which can lead to administrative difficulties if the nurse is not careful to take the name and address of the patient's first wife. Subsequent wives are not recognized legally in the United Kingdom but where visiting in hospital is concerned, they should be extended the courtesy of wifely status (*see also* Clothing; Children; Birth; Marriage; Death).

4. RELIGIONS AND RELIGIOUS FACTORS

This part is arranged in the form of an alphabetical index.

Baha'i

The Baha'i faith was born into the Shi'ih Muslim environment of Iran where it developed at a time of religious unrest. It is a religion that is increasing rapidly especially among British, European and American students. It now has followers throughout the world and has a consultative status with the Economic and Social Council of the United Nations.

Basic beliefs

The Baha'i faith comes from the teachings of Mirza Hussayn Ali, a nobleman who was born in Iran in 1817. He is known to his followers as Baha'u'llah which means the Glory of God. His forerunner or Herald Siyyid Ali Muhammad, known as the Bab (Gate) forecast a new age and it was his declaration in Shiraz in May 1844 that is commemorated as the birth-date of the Baha'i religion.

Christians, Jews, Muslims and Zoroastrians have quarrelled frequently. So the need for peace and unit between different religions is now reflected in Baha'u'llah's teachings.

His followers believe that there is one God and that all the prophets, such as Buddha, Jesus Christ, Mohammed and the founders of all the world religions, are prophets of the same God working towards a united world religion; the different religions and peoples of the world are therefore striving towards the same end, and religion must also go hand in hand with science to produce a peaceful world.

The Baha'i community encourages equality between men and women and condemns prejudice, whether religious, racial, class or national. It seeks to ensure compulsory education for everyone, including the adoption and teaching of an auxiliary universal language. It also aims to eliminate extremes of wealth and poverty. Its followers would like to see universal peace achieved by a federal world government which would deal with problems of a global nature; national governments would carry out decisions within their own countries.

Religious observances and articles

A patient may request a Baha'i prayer book or a small pamphlet such as *The Message of Baha'u'llah*, published by the Baha'i Publishing Trust. Such publications may be obtained from the local Baha'i community.

Minister of religion

The local spiritual assembly of the Baha'is may be contacted by referring to the local telephone directory or yellow pages. If there appears to be no local group, then contact the London headquarters of the Baha'i faith, who will find a member of the Baha'i community to visit the patient.

Attitudes to aspects of care

There are no special requirements as far as clothing and diet are concerned. Drugs are allowed if prescribed. Alcohol is forbidden, but it can be permitted if two qualified medical practitioners state that there is no alternative and that it is the essential basis of a medicine. There are no particular attitudes to the control of pain, except that the same restrictions apply to the use of narcotics as those outlined for alcohol. Apart from a general modesty, the Baha'i have no special views about their bodies or hair.

Treatment

Consent to treatment is no different from the local legal requirements of the cultural group from which a believer originates, and the Baha'i faith have no objection to spare part or transplant surgery, or to the giving or receiving of blood transfusions.

The termination of pregnancy can only be contemplated if the life of the mother is at stake — but not for social reasons, as it is believed that the soul of a child exists from the moment of conception.

Family planning is a question of individual conscience, but at the same time followers believe that the major purpose of marriage is to raise children.

Terminal care, last offices and burial

Baha'i prayers are read if the patient is unable to recite them himself.

When a member of the Baha'i community dies he is washed and wrapped in a shroud of silk or cotton. A special Baha'i ring (available from the Baha'i Publishing Trust) is placed on a finger, and the body is put in a coffin of crystal, stone or hard fine wood (usually the latter).

The body must be buried (not cremated) within one hour's journey of the place where death occurs. At the interment a special prayer is read. The special ring and prayer are not essential for children under 15 years old.

Relationships with others

The Baha'i treat women and children as equals and are very tolerant toward other religions and cultures, because they regard them as having one origin. They have no objection to associating with others but, when they die, they would rather not be buried in a communal grave containing people of other religions.

Further reading

Esslemont, *Baha'u'llah and the New Era*
Baha'i Prayer Book
Huddleston, *This Earth is but One Country*
Gleanings from the Writings of Baha'u'llah
Prayers and Meditations of Baha'u'llah
M. Perkins and P. Hainsworth, *The Baha'i Faith*, Ward Lock Educational, London, 1980.

Pamphlets
The Baha'i Faith
Life after Death
The Messengers of God are One
The Mission of Baha'u'llah
The Message of Baha'u'llah
All these pamphlets are available from the Baha'i Publishing Trust, 2 South Street, Oakham, Rutland, Leics LE15 6HY.

Buddhism

Buddhism is the major religion in the following countries: Burma, Bhutan, Nepal, Sikkim, Sri Lanka, Thailand and Tibet.

Basic beliefs

Buddhism is based on the teaching of Siddhartha Gautama the Buddha (Figure 2) who lived in the sixth century BC in what is now Nepal. Some Buddhist scholars, however, argue that Buddhism is more a way of living than a religion as it acknowledges no God or gods.

Buddhist teaching is based on non-violence and brotherhood. Buddhists adhere to the idea of *karma* (hard work) but for the Buddhist this is a matter of action which must be related to rebirth. Buddhists believe in reincarnation which means that an individual has lived many lives before and that, after death, he or she goes on to a future life. Whatever a person does in this life influences his or her next incarnation and so, in each life, man learns from the experiences of the past and should progress towards perfection or *nirvana*. To achieve *nirvana*, which is an infinite state of perfection, total selflessness is required, with an absence of separateness and suffering. One must follow the eightfold path which stems from the four noble truths.

The four noble truths

The four noble truths can lead man by his own efforts to enlightenment.

Figure 2 The Buddha

The *first* is that all living things are characterized by suffering and un-happiness. The *second* is that it is wrong desire and selfishness that has caused this suffering. The *third* is that if one removes wrong desire and selfishness one then eliminates suffering and unhappiness. The *fourth* is that the way to remove wrong desire and selfishness is to adhere to the eightfold path to enlightenment.

The eightfold path

This is a lifelong practice which the Buddhists believe is in eight steps or phases.

Step 1   The Buddhist must have a complete understanding of life.

Step 2   He must have the right outlook and motives.

Step 3   He must have right speech, in other words, he must not lie or gossip.

Step 4   He must carry out 'perfect conduct' which involves being and doing good as well as ceasing to be and to do evil. This includes the Buddhist belief that one must be careful not to take life. In all actions, the Buddhist should refrain from extremes. He must not be dishonest, deceitful or a thief.

Step 5   He must earn his livelihood in a manner appropriate to Buddhist teaching.

Step 6   He must make the right effort which means that he must develop self-discipline.

Step 7   He must have right-mindfulness; this requires mental exercises in self-awareness and concentration.

Step 8   He must have right meditation. The Buddhist may meditate on subjects such as self-analysis, philosophy and Buddhist teaching until, ultimately, consciousness is raised beyond what is usually experienced by the human mind. The techniques of concentration and meditation in Buddhism are very like those of Raja Yoga (see Hinduism, p. 70).

Schools of Buddhism

The two major schools of Buddhism are geographically divided but co-exist peacefully. They are: the Southern School, the Theravada or Teaching of the Elders, which is found in Burma, Laos, Kampuchea, Sri Lanka, Thailand and parts of India; and the Northern or Mahayana School which is found in Korea, China, Japan, Tibet, Nepal and South Mongolia.

The Theravada School   This is sometimes known by critics as *Hinayana* or Lesser Vehicle which seems to imply that it is more rigid and less rich than other Buddhist teaching. The Theravada School adheres strictly to the original teaching of the Buddha, as recorded in the earliest extant texts.

The Mahayana School   This is sometimes referred to as the Greater Vehicle; however, it appears to many Buddhists to have gone to the opposite extreme and adopted many unorthodox practices.

ZEN BUDDHISM

Zen Buddhism developed largely in Japan following the teachings of Eisai who in the twelfth century went to China to study this particular form of meditative Buddhism. Zen embodies many practices which are incongruous in other Buddhist schools. For example, there are techniques to perfect the arts of archery, fencing, other martial arts and flower arrangement, of which the development of the tea ceremony and the ancient Samurai warrior are typical. Zen Buddhism also provides an intellectual and very disciplined form of Buddhism which has a growing following in the west. It is further divided into the Rinzai and the Soto Zen sects; both are Japanese in origin and have groups in the United Kingdom.

The Rinzai sect

This sect follows the teaching of Eisai, stresses the study of sutras and continues to develop new techniques in meditation.

The Soto Zen sect

The Soto form of Zen Buddhism was introduced by a follower of Eisai called Dogen, and emphasises sitting meditation.

Festivals

In the Theravada School the most important festival is Buddha day. This is the anniversary chosen to celebrate the Buddha's birth, enlightenment and death, and takes place in spring at full moon.

Religious observances and articles

All the Buddhist requires is an opportunity to meditate without interruption at various times throughout the day. The length of time for meditation is a matter of personal choice. A patient may wish to have a small statue of the Buddha beside him.

Minister of religion

There are no ministers of religion as such but a patient may welcome a visit from a Buddhist monk if there is one nearby. If there is not one locally contact the Buddhist Society in London who should be able to give the address of a local contact.

Attitudes to aspects of care

Attitudes are not very different from those of British society in general with regard to the body, hair and diet, except that some Buddhists are vegetarians, and some also abstain from alcohol. Pain is accepted with as little complaint as possible.

Treatment

Consent to treatment for a Buddhist is no different from British legal requirements. There is no objection to spare part surgery and transplant surgery nor to the giving and receiving of blood. However, many Buddhists object strongly to the termination of pregnancy and contraception.

Terminal care, last offices and burial

There is no special form of observance or rite for the dying but the patient should be visited by a Buddhist monk and, if possible, one from his own particular school. Buddhists traditionally request cremation.

Relationships with others

Buddhists respect the old and young alike and are very tolerant towards other religious sects and nationalities. They treat women as equals although this may be influenced by the cultural traditions of their own countries.

Further reading

The following are available from the Buddhist Society.
C. Humphreys, *Basic Buddhism.*
F. L. Woodward, *Some Sayings of the Buddha.*
D. T. Suzuki, *What is Zen?*
R. Walpola, *What the Buddha Taught.*
S. Shumryn, *Zen Mind: Beginner's Mind.*

Christianity

For practical purposes, there are three major groups within the Christian Church. They are, in alphabetical order, the Orthodox Church, the Protestant Church and the Roman Catholic Church. Each of these three groups can be further divided into denominations and sects.

Other sects which can be regarded as offshoots from Christianity are dealt with on pages 91–101, and include Jehovah's Witnesses, Mormons, Spiritualists and Unitarians.

Basic beliefs

Each of the three major groups have many tenets of faith in common.

First, all the major Christian groups believe in the historical Jesus of Nazareth, who was born in Bethlehem nearly 2000 years ago. The majority of these groups also believe that his birth in a stable was a virgin birth although some are less emphatic about this than others.

Most of the teaching and the healing miracles of Jesus took place during the last three years of life in what is now Israel, Jordan and Syria. The area was under Roman occupation at the time under the governorship of Pontius Pilate.

Jesus was born into a Jewish family and community. His followers believed him to be the Jewish Messiah, 'the Anointed One' who would lead and redeem the people of Israel. In Greek, the word for Messiah is Christ, hence the name Jesus Christ and the term 'Christian'.

Following the opposition of those who felt threatened by the great following he had, and influenced by the political background of the Roman occupation, Jesus Christ was crucified by the Romans in approximately AD 33 just outside Jerusalem. The essence of the Christian belief can be summed up in the Apostle's Creed.

> I believe in God the Father Almighty, Creator of heaven and earth: and in Jesus Christ his only Son, our Lord who was conceived by the Holy Spirit, born of the Virgin Mary; suffered under Pontius Pilate, was crucified, dead and buried, he descended into hell; the third day he rose again from the dead, he ascended into heaven; is seated at the right hand of God the Father Almighty; from thence he shall come to judge the quick and the dead. I believe in the Holy Ghost; the holy Catholic Church; the Communion of Saints; the Forgiveness of sins; the Resurrection of the body, and the life of the world to come. Amen.

Other important passages of Christ's teaching come from the Sermon on the Mount (*Matthew* 5–7; *Luke* 6:20ff) and the Lord's Prayer (*Matthew* 6:9; *Luke* 11:1).

The Christian Church was started after his death by Christ's twelve apostles. The history of the early Church can be found in the *Acts of the Apostles* and in the *Letters of St Paul* to the early Christian churches.

Above all, Christians believe in a loving, just and personal God who lived as man and was crucified for the sins of mankind but who was resurrected from the grave. They also believe that the salvation of mankind lies through following Jesus Christ, the son of God.

Principal festivals of the Christian Church

Christmas   This is the feast of the birth of Christ and is celebrated on 25 December except in the Orthodox Church when it is later. In most Christian countries it is a family occasion involving the giving and receiving of gifts.

Lent   Lent lasts for approximately six weeks (40 days) beginning on Ash Wednesday and ending on Good Friday. It celebrates Christ's 40 days in the desert. It is a time for reflection when many Christians forego pleasures of one kind or another and try, in a positive way, to be better people. Nurses may find that patients have 'given up' something well-loved for Lent, such as foods, alcohol or smoking.

Good Friday This falls at the end of Lent and is a solemn day in the church, as it marks the day on which Christ was crucified. (The dates for Good Friday and Easter vary each year but they usually fall in the month of March or April. The Orthodox Church celebrates Easter at a different time from the Protestant and Roman Catholic churches.)

Easter Day This is the most important festival in the Christian Church and should be a very joyful occasion, as it is the day on which Christians celebrate Christ's resurrection from the dead.

Whitsun (Pentecost) Whitsun corresponds to the Jewish feast of Pentecost. Its significance for Christians is that it was during the feast of Pentecost, following Christ's death, that the Holy Spirit came among Christ's apostles and followers enabling them to communicate with the crowds in a variety of languages.

The Orthodox Church

The Orthodox Church is found throughout the world. It developed in the sixth century AD when the Patriarch in Constantinople began to differ from the Roman Catholic Church over matters of doctrine. The final break with the Roman Catholic Church, however, came in the eleventh century AD when the Pope excommunicated the Patriarch of Constantinople (now Istanbul).

The Orthodox Church had for centuries been greatly influenced by the Byzantine Empire. This is shown very strikingly in the architecture of Greek, Eastern and Russian Orthodox churches and in the beautiful icons they venerate.

The Orthodox Church does not recognize the Pope as the successor to St Peter nor does it believe the Pope to be infallible. On matters of doctrine it shares the basic beliefs outlined above, but one of the major differences is that the Orthodox Church does not agree with the *filioque* clause in the Nicene Creed which they consider to be a totally unjustifiable addition. The filioque clause refers to the notion that the Holy Ghost proceeds from the Father and the Son.

Like the Roman Catholic Church the Orthodox Church believes in transubstantiation — that is, when the Communion bread and wine are consecrated they become the true physical Body of Christ.

There are four Patriarchates in the Orthodox Church — Alexandria, Antioch, Constantinople (Istanbul) and Jerusalem; they are the oldest and are held in special esteem by the members of the Orthodox Church.

In addition there are eleven autocephalous churches — those of Albania, Bulgaria, Cyprus, Czechoslovakia, Georgia, Greece, Poland, Rumania, Russia, Serbia and Sinai.

The Orthodox Church is worldwide; branches can be found in China, Finland, Japan, South America, the United Kingdom, the United States and western Europe.

THE RUSSIAN ORTHODOX CHURCH

The basic beliefs are as those outlined for other Orthodox Churches above.

Religious observances and articles

Patients may request a copy of the Holy Bible, a book of orthodox prayers and a crucifix. Some may wish to hear extracts from the Orthodox Liturgy read to them or from a cassette recording. Some patients may bring in a small family icon. This may cause problems as they are very beautiful and sought-after works of art, quite apart from their religious significance, and there is a risk in hospital that they may be lost, damaged or stolen. It is advisable, therefore, for the patient's family to keep it in safe custody but bring it to the patient whenever he wishes to see it.

Minister of religion

Contact the local Russian Orthodox Church, or the Russian Orthodox Church in London (the telephone number is in the Central London yellow pages).

Attitudes to care

There are no special attitudes held by the Russian Orthodox Church regarding the body, hair or clothing apart from the desire for privacy and modesty.

There are no particular dietary requirements. However, there are days when Orthodox Christians must fast. For patients in hospital the patient and staff should be able to reach a reasonable compromise.

Orthodox Christians may drink alcohol in moderation and take all drugs prescribed by a doctor, but the Orthodox Church is totally opposed to the taking of drugs for other than strictly medical purposes. While commending a patient's fortitude in bearing pain the Orthodox Church leaves it to the patient and his doctor to decide on the question of painkilling analgesia.

Treatment

There are no special difficulties regarding consent to treatment. The Russian Orthodox Church is indifferent to the question of spare part and transplant surgery believing it to be a matter for the patient and doctor to decide between them. Contraception and blood transfusion are also acceptable. Termination of pregnancy, however, is only permissible on strictly medical grounds and not for social reasons.

Terminal care, last offices and burial

The local Russian Orthodox parish priest should be consulted and invited to visit the patient. The priest will usually hear the patient's confession, anoint him with the Oil of the Sick and give him Communion when appropriate.

After death the body is usually taken to lie in an open coffin in the Church where the family and friends of the deceased may pay their last respects.

Further reading

T. Ware, *The Orthodox Church*, Penguin, Harmondsworth, 1969.
S. Hackel, *The Orthodox Church*, Ward Lock Educational, London, 1975.

The Protestant Church

The word protestant developed at the time of Luther in the early sixteenth century. He led the protest against the sale of indulgences and other aspects of the Roman Catholic Church at that time. From then on dissident churches were known as protestant churches. For the purpose of this book the Protestant Church in England and Wales is divided into four separate groups and discussed alphabetically. The groups are:
1. The Anglican Church.
2. Churches which are members of the Free Church Federal Council.
3. Churches whose members are also automatically cared for by the Free Church chaplain.
4. Those churches and groups whose members are normally considered to fall within the responsibility of the Free Church when in hospital.

The situation in Scotland is different since the national church, the Church of Scotland, is Presbyterian and the term 'Free Church' is not used in the same sense as in England and Wales. For the sake of brevity and clarity, however, the Church of Scotland has been included under category (3) above.

Nurses and doctors working in Scotland should familiarize themselves with the variations of practices and belief among the free Presbyterian churches (the Free Church, the United Free Church and the Free Presbyterian Church) as well as with the Protestant churches described in this book. These differences are important in the Highlands of Scotland particularly, but cannot be dealt with within the limitations of this brief survey.

It should be pointed out here that although full-time or part-time chaplains are appointed to care for the needs of patients and staff of their own denomination the situation in hospitals today leans towards an ecumenical team approach. They also visit patients who are perhaps only nominal non-churchgoing members of a denomination.

THE ANGLICAN CHURCH (CHURCH OF ENGLAND)

The Anglican Church was founded during the reformation. Luther had already been making his radical reforms when Henry VIII broke away from the Roman Catholic Church in 1534 over his divorce from Catherine of Aragon and founded the Church of England.

There are now branches of the Anglican Church in many parts of the world. They have different names according to the country, for example, the Church of England, the Episcopal Church in Scotland, the Church of Ireland, and the relationship between these churches and the State varies from place to place, but there is nevertheless a single, worldwide Anglican Communion, with a basic similarity in belief and practices.

The major organizational differences between the Anglican Church and the Roman Catholic Church, from which it originated, are that it does not acknowledge the Pope as its head nor does it have a college of cardinals. The reigning monarch of the United Kingdom and the Commonwealth is the Supreme Governor of the Anglican Church; the Primate of All England, the Archbishop of Canterbury, is its spiritual leader. Unlike in the Roman Catholic Church, clergy in the Anglican Church may marry.

Basic beliefs

The basic beliefs of the Anglican Church are outlined at the beginning of the section on Christianity but the Anglican Church has not only been influenced by the Roman Catholic Church but also by the Free Churches. Some Anglican Churches such as the Anglo-Catholic or High Church have very elaborate services but it is also possible to find churches holding very simple services with the minimum of ceremony, which are called Low Church.

There is much less emphasis on the role of the Virgin Mary in the Anglican Church than in the Roman Catholic Church. For example, Anglicans do not pray to the Virgin Mary nor to the saints in the hope that they will intercede on their behalf. Anglicans usually address their prayers to God or through Jesus Christ.

Unlike the Orthodox and Roman Catholic Churches, the Anglican Church does not believe in transubstantiation. It regards the consecrated Communion bread and wine as being symbolic of the Body and Blood of Christ but it does not believe that the bread and wine actually *become* the Body and Blood of Christ.

Religious observances and articles

The sacraments — Baptism, Confession, Holy Communion, Laying on of Hands and Anointing — should be available to the patient if he requires them. Marriage can also be arranged by special licence in certain circumstances (see also the section on marriage in part 3, page 40).

If a child is very ill and its life is in danger a nurse may baptise him in the absence of a priest in charge or chaplain. All that needs to be done is to take a small bowl of water, dip a finger into it and with the wet finger make the sign of the cross on the child's forehead saying 'I baptise you (name) in the Name of the Father and of the Son and of the Holy Ghost. Amen.' It is important to inform the vicar or chaplain afterwards.

The patient may ask for a copy of the Holy Bible and the Book of Common Prayer. There are also prayer cards available in most hospital chapels. If the patient wishes to receive Holy Communion the hospital chaplain should be informed. If the patient is ambulant he should be taken to the Chapel five or ten minutes before the service starts so that he can spend a few moments in quiet thought and prayer before the service begins.

If Holy Communion is being brought to the ward, it will help the chaplain if the patient is ready to receive it (for instance, not in the middle of a blanket bath!). It would also help if ambulant patients receiving Communion in the ward could gather near the bed of a bed-fast patient so that a joint Communion can be held. A small side table should be placed beside the bed and a decanter of water placed on it. This is often all that is required because, nowadays, the chaplain usually brings everything with him — but this can vary from hospital to hospital.

Minister of religion

If the patient is in his own home, then contact the local vicar. If he is in hospital, there should be a full-time or part-time Church of England chaplain. The appointment of hospital chaplains depends on the size of the hospital and on the statistical average of patients of a particular church in the hospital. The chaplain visits the sick and their relatives in the hospital. He holds services and administers the sacraments, and he may also broadcast the services on hospital radio. Church of England chaplains are specially trained by the Hospital Chaplaincies Council and the Joint Committee on Chaplaincy. A member of the Anglican clergy may be addressed as 'Mr' or 'Father', as preferred, but it is always wrong to call him 'Reverend'.

The Church Army

The Church Army is an Anglican missionary organization which, rather like the Salvation Army, has officers and sisters. Church Army personnel wear a distinctive grey uniform. In addition to their work with local churches and social work, they visit the sick in hospital.

Attitudes to aspects of care

There are no particular attitudes to clothing, diet, the body, hair and pain other than the dietary ones mentioned in the paragraph on Lent (page 54). Drugs should be for medicinal purposes only, and alcohol should be taken in moderation.

Treatment

There are no differing attitudes in consent to treatment, spare part and transplant surgery, blood transfusions or family planning from those prevailing in British culture. Many Anglicans are totally against terminatin of pregnancy, although the Church does not oppose it if it is on purely medical grounds — for example, to save the mother's life or in the case of a severely deformed fetus.

Terminal care, last offices and burial

There are no last rites in the Anglican Church but the patient should be given an opportunity to have the Church of England chaplain with him when he is dying. Some may ask for Holy Communion. The chaplain can also help to comfort the family and friends of the dying patient. Members of the Church of England may be cremated or buried.

Further reading

A Handbook on Hospital Chaplaincy, Hospital Chaplaincies Council of the General Synod, 1978.

M. Wilson, The Hospital – A Place of Truth, University of Birmingham, 1971.

P. Speck, Loss and Grief in Medicine, Baillière-Tindall, London, 1978.

THE FREE CHURCH

There are many denominations within the Free Church. Other terms for the Free Church are the Non-Conformist, Non-Established Church and Protestant Church. The Churches which make up the Free Church have their origins in the Reformation. Martin Luther and his followers founded the Lutheran Church in the early sixteenth century; other sixteenth-century leaders during the Reformation were Zwingli in Zurich, Calvin in France and John Knox in Scotland.

Anabaptists were also to be found in Switzerland at this time. They were not tolerated and were actively persecuted. As a result they moved to other countries and later went on to found the strong Baptist movements of Canada, Holland, Russia, the United Kingdom and the United States. Baptists can also be found in the USSR today.

In France the Huguenots were the radical protestants. In Scotland, the Church of Scotland, a Presbyterian and Calvinist Church, was founded by John Knox. North America became the refuge of many radical protestants. Many Lutherans, Calvinists, Baptists, Huguenots, etc, went to live in America where they found peace and little opposition. Among them were a group of English Puritans who became known as 'the Pilgrim Fathers'.

In the seventeenth century the Quakers were founded by George Fox and they too emigrated to America. The Order of Amish also developed in America (mainly in Pennsylvania) and still exists today; it is a sect which rejects all forms of modern living including modern dress, electricity and modern machinery.

In the eighteenth century another series of breakaway groups, this time from the Church of England, was led mainly by John Wesley, who founded the Methodist Church. Wesley was followed by his contemporary George Whitefield.

Other sects have developed, including the Seventh Day Adventists, Christadelphians, the Salvation Army, Pentecostalists, and so on, all from the more evangelistic and ecstatic forms of Free Church expression. Members of these various Free Church denominations can be found throughout the world.

The fundamental difference between the Free Church and the Orthodox, Roman Catholic and Anglican Churches lies in the government of church affairs. There is not the same emphasis on hierarchy that one sees in the Episcopalian churches. The Free Church claims to be more democratic with much greater involvement of the congregation in the running of the church.

The architecture of the churches and the form of service is much more simple in style than in the other churches. The prayers and form of service are often spontaneous, but this varies between the different constituent bodies.

Churches which make up the Free Church Federal Council

The Free Church Federal Council was formed in 1940, and is a unity of several individual churches. Those represented by the Free Church Federal Council are:

The Baptist Union of Great Britain and Ireland
The Churches of Christ
The Congregational Federation
The Countess of Huntingdon's Connexion
The Independent Methodist Churches
The Methodist Church
The Moravian Church
The Presbyterian Church of Wales
The Salvation Army
The Union of Welsh Independents

The United Reformed Church
The Wesleyan Reform Union

The churches represented by the Free Church Federal Council have a few individual differences which will be outlined separately, but they are united in their fundamental belief in God and the divinity of Jesus Christ.

Religious observances and articles

A patient may ask for a copy of the Holy Bible and to see the Free Church chaplain. When receiving Holy Communion, many Free Church members are used to receiving the wine in individual glasses and not from a common chalice.

Minister of religion

Patients from any of the churches represented by the Free Church Federal Council have access to the Free Church chaplain in hospital. The chaplain will try to arrange a visit from the patient's own minister, if he so wishes. Those being nursed at home should be seen by their own local minister. In England and Wales the Free Church chaplain is usually part-time. In Scotland, the Church of Scotland chaplain is usually full-time, since the number of patients from that particular denomination is higher than any other.

If the Free Church chaplain is also a member of the Salvation Army he usually wears a badge on his uniform to show that he is available to all Free Church patients and not just to the Salvation Army.

Attitudes to care

The Free Church has no special requirements as to clothing, diet, pain, the body and hair. Some Free Church members do not drink alcohol.

Treatment

Free Church members leave all matters relating to spare part and transplant surgery, termination of pregnancy, family planning and blood transfusions to the conscience of the individual patient.

Terminal care, last offices and burial

There are no special rites practised by the Free Church. A patient belonging to one of the Free Churches should be seen by the Free Church chaplain regularly, and especially as he nears the end of his life. His family too should be seen by the chaplain and offered such help as they require.

It may be helpful to look very briefly at the background of some of the members of the Free Church Federal Council.

The Baptist Union of Great Britain and Ireland (174 578*) The Baptist Church flourished in Rhode Island, USA after the earlier days of persecution as Anabaptists in Europe. It then filtered back into Britain and Ireland. The most significant difference between Baptists and some other Christian groups is that Baptists hold a firm belief in adult baptism by total immersion of the new member in water. Children are not baptised in the Baptist Church, which is traditionally a very evangelical church. One of its famous literary figures was John Bunyan who wrote *A Pilgrim's Progress*.

The Congregational Federation (10 429*) The Congregational Church was founded in the second half of the sixteenth century. Members were originally called independents and laid great emphasis on the part played by the local congregation in ordering its own affairs. In 1972 the Congregational Church of England and Wales united with the Presbyterian Church of England to form the United Reformed Church.

The Countess of Huntingdon's Connexion (675*)

The Methodist Church (516 798*) The Methodist Church was founded by John Wesley in the mid-eighteenth century, as a breakaway movement from the established Church of England. Many of the traditions of Church of England worship can be seen in the Methodist form of service.

The Moravian Church (2700*)

The Salvation Army William Booth founded the Salvation Army in 1865, helped by his wife, Catherine, to wage a war on behalf of Christianity against evil in all its forms including human misery and social injustice.

The Salvation Army was among the leaders in recognizing and acting upon occupational health hazards. At the end of the nineteenth century William Booth set up a match factory which did not use phosphorus in protest against those manufacturers who continued to use it despite its effect on the workers' health. He also set up employment exchanges. The Salvation Army continues this work vigorously by helping the destitute, the lonely, the poor and the starving. It also runs a missing persons bureau.

Many people view the Salvation Army as a social agency made up of people in an unusual uniform frequently accompanied by brass bands

* Membership statistics taken from *The Free Church Federal Council Report for 1979 and Directory for 1980*, page 27.

and tambourines. This is certainly true, but the Salvation Army is first and foremost a worldwide Christian denomination.

Basic beliefs

The Salvation Army is evangelical, with a strong emphasis on personal conversion and living a Christian life of service to God. Salvationists view service to God as service to Man, and emphasize the joy of service to God and Man.

Religious observances and articles

The Salvation Army emphasizes the inward nature of spiritual belief, so does not encourage the practice of the sacraments of Baptism and Holy Communion.

The patient may request a visit from the Free Church chaplain or the nearest Salvation Army Officer. He may also like a copy of the Holy Bible if his own is unavailable.

Attitudes to aspects of care

Salvationists wear a distinctive uniform but this will not affect them in hospital. They have no dietary taboos except that alcohol is completely forbidden and should therefore be avoided in any ingestible form.

Attitudes to treatment

Salvationists have no particular requirements for consent to treatment and they find blood transfusion, spare part and transplant surgery acceptable.

The Salvation Army advises that the termination of pregnancy should be avoided and counsels carrying the fetus to term, while giving all possible supportive help. Contraception is acceptable, although Salvationists refrain from embryocidal methods.

Terminal care, last offices and burial

Although there are no specific rites and ceremonies, Salvationists appreciate being visited by fellow Salvationists and the Free Church chaplain.

Relationships with others

Salvationists are tolerant of other races and religions, and the Salvation Army avoids party politics so that it can continue its campaigning work with any government.

Further reading

R. Rollier, *The General Next to God*, Collins Fontana, London, 1968.
C. W. Kew, *The Salvation Army*, Religious Education Press Pergamon, Oxford, 1977.

The United Reformed Church   Great emphasis is laid on the personal responsibility of each member of the church (see also the Congregational Federation).

Further reading

The Free Church Federal Council, *Handbook for Free Church Hospital Chaplains*, Free Church Federal Council, London, 1977.

Churches whose members are also automatically cared for by the Free Church chaplain   There are many other sects which, although not members of the Free Church Federal Council, come under the care of the Free Church chaplain in hospital. They are:

The Church of Scotland
The Plymouth or other Brethren
The Religious Society of Friends (Quakers)

The Church of Scotland   This worldwide religion was founded by John Knox in the mid-sixteenth century.

Basic beliefs

These have already been described under the headings of Christianity and the Free Church.

Religious observances and articles

Patients may ask for a copy of the Holy Bible and a book of paraphrased psalms. Some may also wish to receive Holy Communion.

Minister of religion

The patient may ask to see the Free Church chaplain. (In Scotland there is a full-time Church of Scotland chaplain in most hospitals.) Alternatively he may wish to see his own minister or one of his local church elders, a deacon or a deaconess.

Attitudes to care, treatment, terminal care, last offices and burial

These are outlined in the section on the Free Church Federal Council (page 62).

Further reading

A. Gemmell, *The Hospital Chaplain*, St Andrew's Press, Edinburgh, 1979.

The Plymouth or other Brethren   The Plymouth Brethren, the Exclusive Brethren and other groups of Brethren usually lead a very strict and what may seem to others a restricted life. Members of some of these sects do not mix socially with non-Brethren. They do not watch television, listen to the radio (except for the news), visit concert halls, theatres or go dancing.

Religious observances and articles
The patient may ask for a copy of the Holy Bible.

Minister of religion
Patients may ask to see the Free Church minister but usually prefer a leader from their own sect. Sometimes it is difficult to contact some- one from the sect as they are often without telephones. In most cases the family will organize a visit by members of the sect.

Attitudes to aspects of care
Some Brethren are so strict that they do not even eat meals with non- Brethren and some insist on bringing in their own food. Some patients from these sects do not speak to someone who is not Brethren. It is not always easy to find a nurse who is a member of the sect. The author once encountered a patient from the Brethren who insisted on addressing the bed or the wall instead of the doctor, and would pray loudly to God asking him to send a nurse with a bedpan. This, however, was an exceptional case! When bathing, many of these patients wish to wear some article of clothing as they must never appear naked. Many compromise by wearing something on their head, or a ribbon in the hair.

Treatment
It is unlikely that a member of this sect will accept or even seek termi- nation of pregnancy, nor any family planning which involves the use of artificial methods. However, officially, all these are matters for each individual to decide.

Terminal care, last offices and burial
These matters are treated with the utmost simplicity and the Free Church chaplain should be called.

The Religious Society of Friends (Quakers) The Religious Society of Friends (Quakers) was founded by George Fox in the mid-seventeenth century. The Friends believe that there is 'that of God' in everyone and consider religion to be an inward rather than an outward experience. Friends follow the teaching of Jesus. There is no Quaker form of ser- vice, nor is there a liturgy, or sacraments. Many Friends are pacifists.

Religious observances and articles
The Religious Society of Friends hold their meetings in silence. There-

fore any Friend who is a patient would appreciate opportunities for silence and quiet reflection. They do not use religious symbols but may like a copy of the Holy Bible or some other book of religious writings.

Minister of religion

There is no clergy but there are Overseers of local Friends Meetings. If a Friend wishes to see the local Overseer he can be contacted through the local meeting house. Alternatively the Free Church chaplain should be contacted.

Attitudes to aspects of care

There are no particular differences in the attitudes of Friends to clothing, diet, the body, hair or pain. Some Friends may hesitate to rely on drugs and many abstain from alcohol.

Treatment

Friends will accept spare part surgery, family planning and blood transfusions. Transplant surgery and termination of pregnancy are considered matters of individual conscience.

Terminal care, last offices and burial

There are no special rites involved in the care of a Friend who is terminally ill. However, the patient and his family might appreciate a visit from the Overseer from the local Friends Meeting House.

Further reading

G. H. Gorman, *Introducing Quakers*, Quaker Home Service, London, 1969.

D. Lampden, *Facing Death*, Quaker Home Service, London, 1979.

Roman Catholic Church

The Roman Catholic Church is a worldwide Church based on the teachings of Jesus Christ. It takes its authority from Christ's discussion with the apostle Peter during which Jesus said

> Thou art Peter and upon this rock will I build my Church; and the gates of hell shall not prevail against it. And I will give unto thee the keys of the kingdom of heaven: and whatsoever thou shalt bind on earth shall be bound in heaven; and whatsoever thou shalt loose on earth shall be loosed in heaven (*Matthew* 16: 16—19).

Roman Catholics believe that the Pope is St Peter's historical and spiritual successor and that he is invested with Christ's authority and is, therefore, infallible. The Church is centrally organized in a hierarchy of priests, bishops and cardinals. The supreme head of the Church is the

Bishop of Rome who is the Pope, and the headquarters of the Church is in the Vatican in Rome.

Clergymen in the Western Rites Roman Catholic Church must remain celibate. This rule does not apply to clergymen of the Eastern Rites unless they are bishops or monks. The Roman Catholic Church also has many religious orders of monks and nuns. Some are closed, contemplative orders; others are teaching, nursing and orders for social work.

Basic beliefs

In addition to those outlined above and on page 53 Roman Catholics also attach great importance to the Virgin Mary and the saints, praying to them or asking them to mediate on their behalf in addition to praying directly to God through Jesus Christ.

Prayer, Confession, the Mass (Holy Communion) and other sacraments are all important aspects of the Roman Catholic faith. Roman Catholics also believe in transubstantiation so that when the bread and wine are consecrated, they become the true physical Body and Blood of Christ.

Religious observances and articles

The patient may request Confession, Holy Communion, or the Sacrament of the Sick — sometimes called the Last Rites, Anointing or Extreme Unction. The Sacrament of the Sick is administered when a patient is seriously ill; the priest anoints the patient with oil and prays that God will ease the patient's suffering and forgive him all his sins.

The patient may request a copy of the Holy Bible, a Missal, a rosary, prayer cards, medallions of the Pope or saints or the Virgin Mary and often a statuette of the Virgin Mary or crucifix. Some patients keep a bottle of Holy Water by their beds; some of the Holy Water comes from Lourdes, a shrine in southern France which is considered by many to be a healing shrine where miraculous cures have taken place.

Minister of religion

In hospital there is usually a part-time Roman Catholic chaplain. Otherwise it is best to contact the local Roman Catholic priest.

Attitudes to aspects of care

There are no differing attitudes to care from the point of view of clothing, drugs, alcohol, pain, the body and hair from the majority of people within the same culture.

Although there are now no official restrictions on diet, one may still find many Roman Catholics who do not eat meat on Fridays, in remembrance of Good Friday. Elderly Roman Catholics may be among those who only eat fish on Fridays because it used to be part of the Roman Catholic tradition.

Treatment

There are no differences on the question of consent to treatment and blood transfusions. The Roman Catholic Church has no objection in principle to spare part or transplant surgery. It is, however, totally opposed to the termination of pregnancy, to artificial contraception and sterilization. A devout Roman Catholic can, therefore, only use the rhythm method of birth control.

Terminal care, last offices and burial

The patient should receive the Sacrament of the Sick, which should follow his confession if he is conscious. When performing last offices the family may request that the patient's hands be placed in an attitude of prayer holding a flower, crucifix or rosary.

Further reading

We Live: An Introduction to the Practice of Catholicism Today, Catholic Enquiry Centre, London, 1980.

The Linacre Papers
   (a) *The Principle of Respect for Human Life*
   (b) *Is There a Morally Significant Difference Between Killing and Letting Die?*
   (c) *Ordinary and Extraordinary Means of Prolonging Life*
all published by the Linacre Centre, London.

Confucianism

Confucianism has had a great influence on Chinese thought and culture for centuries and at one time was the established religion of China.

It developed in China in the sixth century BC. Its founder was Confucius (in Chinese K'ung-fu'tzu), who revised many older writings in his five classics which are the *I Ching, Shu Ching, Shih Ching, Li Chi* and *Ch'un Ch'iu*. Confucianism is also based on the Four Books. *Lun Yu*, better known as *The Analects* contains the principles of Confucian philosophy; the other books are *Ta Hsueh, Ching Yung* and *Meng Tzu Shu*.

The basis of Confucianism is belief in a supreme being and in The Way (*Tao*), which is a sense of order, discipline, respect and enlightened self-interest. Confucius developed the concept of *Li* which is concerned with ceremony, ritual and order, and believed that if everyone adhered to the right way of doing things, life would be peaceful and well-ordered. His idea was that society should be like a well-disciplined family with everyone knowing his place and his duty in the order of things. He also taught that a person should do to others only what he would wish them to do to him.

This sense of order and respect is very much part of family and social life among Chinese people and Part 3 on culture (page 31) shows how Confucianism in Chinese culture can affect the approach to care of the elderly in particular.

Confucianism is unlikely to impinge upon the care and treatment of patients in British hospitals but, since it colours very strongly the customs, thoughts and attitudes of all Chinese, regardless of their professed religion, it is further covered in various areas of Part 3.

Hinduism

Hinduism is a very ancient religion, centred mainly in India and Nepal but also found in countries to which Indians have emigrated. It is, for example, not uncommon now in the United Kingdom, in parts of Africa, Sri Lanka and Mauritius. It can also be found in Thailand, Indonesia, Burma and Malaysia.

Basic beliefs

Hinduism has millions of gods and goddesses because Hindus regard a person as an entity, but most Hindus believe that these gods and goddesses are manifestations of one God. The three great gods of Hinduism, who combine to make up the supreme being or God are Brahman the Creator, Vishnu the Preserver and Shiva who combines destruction with the regeneration of life.

Hinduism has no fixed creed and is a very diverse religion — it is, in fact more a way of life than a religion. There are several schools of Hindu philosophical thought and some separate religions have developed from it. Buddhism, for example, developed from Hinduism. The major schools of Hindu philosophy are Samkhya, Yoga, Nyaya, Vaishesika, Purva-Mumamsa and Vedanta. Of these, perhaps the best known in the west is Yoga.

HATHA-YOGA

Yoga is mental, spiritual, moral and physical discipline. Hatha-Yoga is the physical aspect of this discipline. A follower of Hatha-Yoga learns to concentrate and ultimately to meditate while carrying out various physical exercises. There are many followers of Hatha-Yoga in the west as well as in India and Asia, and many of these devotees go on to learn the contemplative and philosophical aspects of this discipline.

VISHNAVITES

Many Hindus that one can meet in the community or in hospitals in Britain are Vishnavites. They worship Vishnu the Preserver and his incarnations as Rama and Krishna. Some believe he will come again in a future incarnation as Kalik when he will bring about the end of the world and destroy evil. In his incarnation as Rama, Vishnu was a good king combining beauty, bravery and justice. As Krishna he was a charming young man who brought with him happiness and fun as well as power and justice.

Most of the teaching of Hinduism comes from the vast amount of Hindu religious literature beginning with the *Vedas* or *Vedic* hymns which are the earliest examples of Hindu literature, written over 4000 years ago. Following the *Vedas* come the *Upanishads* and *Brahmanas*. The *Upanishads* influenced the changes in Hinduism away from the diverse worship of many gods — polytheism — and towards a more unified form of belief in and worship of a supreme being, God. But perhaps the greatest influence on Hindu life and thought came from the *Bhagavad Gita* which in turn comes from the great Hindu epic, the *Mahabharata*. There are two great epics, the other one being the *Ramayana*.

There is no standard form of worship. Some Hindus meditate, some pray, some combine meditation, prayer and physical exercises as in Hatha-Yoga. Some Hindus go to the temple once a week, while others prefer to worship at home and may pray daily. Some Hindus fast once a week. The Hindus firmly believe that a coat which suits one person need not necessarily suit others, so there is little dogma in their religion.

In the home many Hindus keep a small shrine (Figure 3), in which

Figure 3 A Hindu shrine in a home

there is a statue or image of one of the gods or goddesses surrounded by flowers and incense sticks.

Important festivals of Hinduism

Shivatri (in March)   The festival of the god Shiva.

Holi (end of March)   This is a spring festival of Krishna, embodying the gaiety and fun of Krishna in his youth. In this festival coloured powder and water are thrown over everyone.

Ram Naum (April)   Rama's birthday (one of the incarnations of Vishnu).

New Year (mid April).

Rath Yatra (July)   Festival of Jaggarath.

Janam Ashtami (August)   Krishna's birthday (another incarnation of Vishnu).

Ganesh Chaturthi (end of August)   The Festival of Ganesh the god of success and good fortune. Ganesh is seen with the head and trunk of an elephant because it is with his trunk that he removes all obstacles to success.

Durga Purja (October)   The Festival of Kali, Shiva's wife, and often known as Kali the Mother. This is a family festival.

Diwali (mid-October)   The festival of lights, where the goddess of wealth, Lascami, is worshipped. Special lamps are lit and children make paper boats and float candles in them.

REINCARNATION AND TRANSMIGRATION

Hindus believe in reincarnation, so that when they die their soul is re-born again in a new human life. This is because they have to work out their destiny on earth in each subsequent life. Hindus believe that God is approached through knowledge (*jnana*), hard work (*karma*) and devotion (*bhakti*). They also believe that each individual soul goes to make up the supreme soul, and that each individual has to undergo a series of rebirths before he can become part of Brahman. In each life he has his special work to carry out, and this led to the development of the caste system (discussed further in Part 3 on culture, page 43).

Because of the belief in reincarnation and in some cases transmigration (rebirth as an animal, insect, etc.) many very strict Hindus will do almost anything to avoid killing even the smallest insect. However, many of these very strict sects are not found outside India because, for example, very strict Brahmans may not cross the sea.

Religious observances and articles

The patient may wish to meditate or pray to his favourite deity quietly. He may wish to perform some yoga exercises, if possible. He may also wish to read from the *Vedas*, *Upanishads*, *Bhagavad Gita*, *Mahabharata* or *Ramayana*.

Some patients may like to have a small statue or picture of one or more of the Hindu gods or goddesses beside his bed. Some may treasure a small bottle of water from the River Ganges, a holy river for the Hindus.

Minister of religion

The patient's family may wish to contact a local Hindu friend on his behalf. Alternatively he may wish to see the local Hindu priest. The pandit, the title given to Hindu priests, can be located through the local Hindu temple or through the local community relations council (address in the local telephone book).

Attitudes to aspects of care

There are no particular attitudes to clothing other than that Hindus are modest and Hindu women may prefer to wear a sari to traditional western dress.

The body and hair, however is particularly important in the case of women. Hindu women are very reluctant and many refuse, to undress in front of a male nurse or doctor, and frequently prefer to be examined and treated by female doctors. Nor do Hindu women like to expose themselves in short open-back gowns such as operation or X-ray gowns. Longer closed gowns like operating theatre nurses' dresses should be worn if possible or, if the patient is unable to put on such a dress, a long close-fitting operating theatre gown which can be securely tied should be offered to her. Hindu patients prefer showers to a bath.

Long hair is important to Hindu women and a married woman may refuse to have her hair cut without the permission of her husband.

Hindu diet is based on the belief that the cow is a sacred animal and therefore no practising Hindu will eat anything that comes from such cattle, such as beef, veal, sausages, even beef extract. Some are so strict that they do not eat meat or fish at all.

Some Hindus are vegans, and eat nothing that comes from an animal, not even jellies, for example, because they are made from animal gelatine. This group do not wear clothes or shoes made from the skins of animals, such as fur or skin coats, woollen jumpers or blankets, leather clothes or shoes. They may also require a foam pillow as they disapprove of the use of feather pillows.

Indians also have an unusual concept of hot and cold foods. As this idea, although perhaps developed from religion, has become a matter of Indian culture, it is discussed in full in Part 3 on culture (page 28).

Alcohol is not forbidden but should only be taken in moderation. Drugs are acceptable including analgesic agents but they must not come from beef cattle (for example, bovine insulin and some vaccines).

Treatment

The legal requirements for consent to treatment are sufficient but the doctor or nurse may find a female patient unwilling to sign her consent form without consulting her husband or father.

Hindus have no objection to spare part or transplant surgery but, in general, they do not accept bovine grafts. There are no difficulties in relation to blood transfusions.

There is no religious objection to the termination of pregnancy on medical grounds and none to contraception, but health care workers may find that some Asian Hindus find this hard to accept culturally.

Terminal care, last offices and burial

The patient's family may wish to remain near his bedside. They may also insist on the patient's eldest son being present before, at and after the patient's death — even if he is a small child. The family may bring clothes and coins for the patient to touch before they are given to the poor, or read passages from the holy books.

After death relatives, including the eldest son, wash the body (unless it is a woman when the washing is performed by women). Water is often poured into the deceased's mouth. The body is then dressed in new clothes before it leaves the hospital. Hindus may be very reluctant to consent to a post-mortem examination of the body but, if this is unavoidable, many of the traditional procedures described above have to be foregone. After a post-mortem all the organs must be replaced, as Hindus believe that if organs are removed in this way the soul of the deceased will not find peace in the afterlife.

The husband of a deceased Hindu woman cuts the marriage thread placed round her neck at marriage, which must not be removed until the patient dies and then only by her husband. In the event of a post-mortem examination it is a more sensitive gesture to ask the bereaved husband to remove the thread before it takes place.

Hindus prefer cremation to burial except for children under five years of age who should be buried. It is the religious duty of the eldest son to light the funeral pyre, but this is not permitted in Britain where Hindus usually find a symbolic way of fulfilling this religious duty.

JAINISM

One very strict sect which developed from Hinduism is Jainism. There are very few Jains outside India and most are found in Gujarat and southern India; however, a few businessmen are Jains and they travel all over the world.

Jainism is a very austere form of Hinduism. They worship their great teachers of the past such as Mahavira and Parsva. Jains believe in reincarnation and that the only way towards perfection is by transcending the world, by detaching oneself from the world and its pleasures. They abstain from all material pleasure. The most extreme adherents, the Jain monks, are virtually nomads. All Jains believe in *ahimsa*, which is non-violence, and this means not harming any living creature. They strain all fluids before drinking them, especially water. Some wear a mask so that they do not inhale any small creatures, and brush the ground before they tread on it so that no small insect or animal is killed or hurt. They are celibate and strictly vegetarian.

If a Jain is admitted to hospital, he will probably wish to be treated as a strict Hindu with a vegan form of vegetarianism. In addition it may be advisable to contact the local Hindu temple and to ask for a local contact from the India Society, which can give detailed advice and help.

Further reading

K. M. Sen, *Hinduism*, Penguin, Harmondsworth, 1961.

Islam

Islam can be found in almost every country of the world but particularly in Afghanistan, the Arabian Gulf sheikdoms, Egypt, Iran, Iraq, North Africa, Pakistan, Saudi Arabia, Turkey and the USSR.

Basic beliefs

The religion of Islam is followed by Muslims. Islam means submission and Muslims submit themselves to the will of God. In Islam God is called Allah and Muslims believe Him to be the one true God. They follow the teachings of Mohammed whom they regard to be the last great prophet following chronologically after the Jewish prophets and Jesus Christ.

Muslims follow Mohammed's teachings strictly by reading and practising the holy law written in the Koran. Different interpretations of the Koran lead to some of the differences between the varying lifestyles in many Muslim countries and, of course, to the different Islamic sects.

Religious observances and articles

Every day a Muslim should pray to Allah at least five times. Before he says his prayers (*Salah*) he has to perform *Al-Whudhu* (ablution) (see Figure 4).

The process of performing Al-Wudhu is as follows:

Mention the name of Allah by saying 'Bismillah-AR-Rahman-AR-Raheem' (in the name of Allah, the Beneficent, the Merciful).

Wash both hands up to the wrists together three times, ensuring that every part including between the fingers is wetted by water as shown (left)

Taking a handful of water into the mouth, rinse the mouth three times as shown (right)

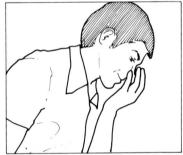

Snuff water contained in the right palm into the nose and then eject the water with the left hand (thrice)

Wash the face, ear to ear, forehead to chin, three times

Figure 4

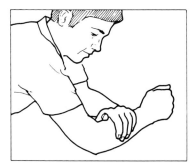

Wash the right arm thoroughly from wrist to elbow three times. Repeat the same with the left hand — as shown (left)

Run moistened hands over the head from forehead to the back and back to the forehead (once)

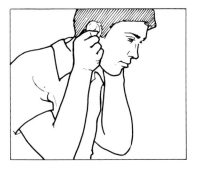

Run moistened fingers through the ears, the first finger of each hand going across the inside of the corresponding ear, while the thumb runs across the outside (once) — as shown (left)

Wash both feet up to the ankles starting from the right and ensuring that all parts particularly between the toes are wetted — as shown (right). If you had performed complete 'Wudhu', before putting on your socks or stockings, it is not necessary to re-remove them when you want to repeat the performance of 'Al-Wudhu'. It is enough to wipe over the stockinged feet with wet hands. This may be done for a period of one day. (and three days on journeys) on the condition that the socks or stockings are never removed.

Muslim ablutions

Salah is performed at the following times:

Fajr — morning
Zuhr — early afternoon
Asr — mid afternoon
Mahgrib — sunset
Isha — night prayer

The exact times of sunrise and sunset are used and many devout Muslims carry a diary or small book giving the exact times for prayer. During *Salah* the Muslim may use a prayer mat and must face towards Islam's most holy shrine the Ka'ba at Mecca.

Special ablutions must be performed after sexual intercourse, nocturnal emissions and childbirth.

Minister of religion

There is no equivalent in Islam to the priest or rabbi of Christianity and Judaism but there are learned men of religion who are called Imams. There are several in Britain especially in London; they can be contacted through the nearest Islamic centre (see the local or London yellow pages), or through the Muslim Information Centre in London.

Attitudes to aspects of care

During a prayer a man must be covered from at least the navel to the knee. Women must be covered from head to foot, and only during a menstrual period are they free from the obligation of *Salah*.

There are no particular official religious taboos about dressing and undressing but many Muslims from the Middle East and Asia have developed very strict attitudes to the dressing and undressing of women. Nurses should be aware of the reluctance of some Muslim women to be undressed or examined in the presence of a man other than their husband. This was discussed above in Part 3 on culture (page 44).

Muslims do not eat any food or ingest any product that may come from a pig; this includes pork, bacon, sausages, ham and some cakes which have been cooked with pig fat. Meat should also be derived from animals that have been ritually slaughtered by a Muslim using the Hallal method. Muslims fast at the festival of Ramadhan, from dawn to sunset, which causes problems for diabetic patients, and may be particularly difficult in the northern hemisphere where the period between sunrise and sunset is so long (northern Scotland, for example). In such cases the local religious leader should be contacted and the matter discussed with both him and the patient (the husband should be included if the patient is a woman). Ill people and the chronically sick, however, have the option of not fasting during Ramadhan although some are reluctant even to take advantage of this dispensation.

Muslims are absolutely forbidden to take drugs or alcohol in any form, although allowances are made for drugs used solely for medical treatment. Once again drugs derived from pigs, such as porcine insulin, are strictly forbidden. Nowadays, some Muslims are not very strict about alcohol. Generally Muslims try to persevere with pain and accept it as God's will. If the patient feels he cannot accept analgesics he may be helped by advice from a relative or a member of the local Islamic centre.

Treatment

There are strong taboos about the termination of pregnancy, and about donating or receiving transplants or grafts. Muslim women are very unlikely to request or accept a termination of pregnancy. Muslims are not permitted to offer their organs for transplant nor to receive a transplanted organ, and they cannot have grafts from material which has come from a pig or from another human, even from another Muslim.

Terminal care, last offices and burial

Special prayers are said for the dying, and all are recited in Arabic, irrespective of nationality or culture. The patient's relatives may wish to recite the prayers or involve Muslims from the nearest Islamic centre or mosque. The prayers which include the declaration of faith: 'There is no God but God and Mohammed is his Messenger', should be recited by the patient if possible and he must face Mecca when doing so.

After death the patient's body is washed according to the Islamic tradition by members of the family. If the body is male it should be washed by men. In some cases it can be washed by women but, except for his wife, the woman must be one who could not have been eligible to marry the man during his life. No man can touch or see a female body after death but any woman can. If a male patient has died and there is no-body available who would normally be allowed to wash the body, *Tayummum* should be performed, which involves washing the hands and face with dust or sand. The male body is then wrapped in three pieces of cloth called a *caffan*. A female body is wrapped in five pieces.

It is of great importance to Muslims that they should be buried, not cremated, as quickly as possible. They also have special burial rites. No body must be buried in a grave deeper than the height of the body. The body is placed in the grave so that it faces Mecca, and the grave must be made up to about 15 cm (6 in) above the ground so that no one can walk on it. Coffins are not acceptable in Islam. Autopsies are also forbidden but each patient's condition and the reason for an autopsy should be discussed with the patient's relatives. Organ donations are strictly forbidden.

Members of the primary care team or ward staff advising relatives can obtain help and advice about last offices and Muslim undertakers from the Muslim Information Centre or from the nearest Islamic centre.

Relationships with others

Muslims recognize Jews and Christians as followers of divinely revealed religions and therefore have much in common with them. However, the history of relationships with Hindus, Buddhists and others, who follow religions which Muslims do not accept as divinely revealed, has been difficult and often violent. Nurses should be aware that a Muslim patient may feel disturbed by the presence of someone from one of these religions in the next bed. It would therefore be more tactful, and welcome to both parties, to separate them.

Muslims from some countries have a different attitude to women from the one which prevails in the west. This is discussed above in Part 3 (page 44). As Muslims often come from very close families support for the sick or bereaved is usually very good.

Further reading

J. S. Idris, *Islam — The Basic Truths*, Muslim Welfare House, London, 1978.

Muslim Education Trust, *Third Primer of Islam — Salah*, London, 1978.

Community Relations Commission, 'Muslim Burials — A policy paper', London, 1975.

MUSLIM SECTS

Muslims endeavour to follow the teaching of Mohammed as laid down in the Koran but inevitably there are different interpretations of it particularly in so far as politics and law are concerned. Some sects are more austere than others, although differences are often more cultural than religious. Nevertheless the nurse should be aware that there are several sects of which the largest and perhaps the most influential are the Sunni, Shi'ih, Ismaili and Wahhabi. The sect may be as important to the patient as the fact that he is a Muslim, and offending sectarian feelings should also be avoided.

Judaism

Judaism is an ancient religion dating from more than 2000 years before the birth of Christ. It is of significance for many other religions, and especially for the Christian faith, in developing and expanding the idea of one God. The history of Judaism is not just a history of a religion but of a people with a unique culture descended from the ancient Hebrew tribes. Great leaders emerged from these nomadic tribes who wandered through the Middle Eastern desert — leaders to the Jews, Muslims and Christians alike — the patriarchs Abraham, Isaac and Jacob and the prophets Moses, Isaiah and Elijah. The history of the Jews has been one of dispersion and persecution; in recent times this led to an active interest in Zionism and the foundation of the State of Israel in 1948, although Zionism was described in the Bible, for example in *Psalms* 122, 125, 126 and 137.

Basic beliefs

The history of Judaism and much of the basis for its doctrine and beliefs can be found in the Old Testament of the Holy Bible. In particular the Law of the Jewish people is in the Torah which is found in the Pentateuch forming the first five books of the Old Testament. Following this comes 'the Prophets' which include the books of *Joshua, Kings, Isaiah, Jeremiah* and others.

Jews believe in one God, referred to as Adonai because the names of God were not pronounced other than by the High Priest in the Temple once a year and is now not known. They believe in the Law as it was given to Abraham and Moses. They await the Messiah, not believing that Jesus of Nazareth was that Messiah, the anointed one who would lead and redeem the people of Israel.

Down the ages rabbis and other great leaders of the Jewish faith have expanded, clarified and further defined the Law and the Prophets. These writings make an enormous work called the Talmud, which, for example, brings into focus Jewish teaching on ethics and ritual. So it is from the strict interpretation of the Pentateuch and the Talmud that Jewish religious observances and festivals derive.

The important Jewish festivals

Rosh Hashanah (Jewish New Year)
Yom Kippur (the Day of Atonement)
Succoth (Feast of Tabernacles)
Simchath Torah (Rejoicing in the Law)
Chanukah (the Feast of Esther)
Purim (the Feast of Esther)
Pesach (the Passover)
and Tishah B'Av (mourning for the destruction of the Temple).

These festivals are common to both Liberal and Orthodox Judaism unless otherwise specified.

It is difficult to give permanent dates, as the Jewish calendar is based on the lunar year and is therefore shorter. Seven times in every nineteen years an extra month is added to adjust the loss. Dates for key festivals can be provided by the Jewish community.

Rosh Hashanah (Jewish New Year) The first ten days of the Jewish New Year are very solemn, being a time of self-analysis and repentance. The Jewish calendar is different from the Christian one. New Year for the Jews takes place in September and in 1982 it will be 5742 until September 1983 when it becomes 5743.

Yom Kippur (Day of Atonement) Yom Kippur takes place on the tenth day of the Jewish New Year, and is the holiest day in the year for the Jews, who must fast for 24 hours. It is a day for each individual to atone for his sins and to resolve to mend his ways. In Biblical times this was the only day on which the High Priest could enter the Temple's Holy of Holies. In modern times it is a day when all devout Jews go to the synagogue and must do no work. Patients will wish to fast on that day, if their health permits.

Succoth (the Feast of Tabernacles) Traditionally this feast lasts nine days. During this time feast huts are erected in the garden, if possible, and the family eats in the hut during the week. The hut is made of branches, without any nails, and with the stars visible at night. The first two and last two days of this festival are holy days of public worship (the *whole* period is for rejoicing), and the feast celebrates the 40 years which the Jews spent in the wilderness. Succoth starts five days after Yom Kippur.

Simchath Torah (Rejoicing in the Law) During the year the whole of the Pentateuch is read in the synagogue in weekly instalments. At a very pleasant and happy ceremony the cycle restarts with Simchath Torah. The last verses of *Deuteronomy* are read, and the cycle begins again with the first verses of *Genesis*.

Chanukah (Festival of Lights) This festival is full of fun for children, and comes in December near to the Christian Christmas. It lasts for eight days and by tradition candles are lit, one on each day of the festival, the candles being placed in the window. This festival celebrates the rededication of the Temple in Jerusalem.

Purim (the Feast of Esther) This is a very happy festival with a party atmosphere which celebrates (in March) the story of Esther, who rescued her people from a plan to kill them in Persia over 2000 years ago.

Pesach (the Passover) This comes in March or April, around the Christian Easter time. It lasts about eight days and during this time no leavened bread is allowed in the house. The Passover is celebrated by a meal in the family home (Figure 5). This is a traditional meal which includes telling the story of the promise made by God to Moses and Aaron in Egypt, who were told to have the people ready to leave Egypt and to eat a hasty meal.

They were also told that every Jew had to eat lamb and smear some of its blood on the doorposts, so that when God passed through Egypt in the night killing the firstborn of both man and beast, he would see the blood and pass over their houses, their firstborn would be saved and

Figure 5 A Passover meal

the exodus from Egypt would begin. Traditionally the stories begin with the youngest male child in the house asking 'Why is this night different to all other nights?' A Jewish patient will probably prefer not to eat bread, cake and other 'leavened' foods at this time.

Pentecost This is traditionally held on the fiftieth day (from the second day of Passover) which is the last day of the seven weeks reckoned from 'the day after the Sabbath' (*Leviticus* 23:11−20). This festival is a harvest offering dating from Biblical times when the first fruits were presented in the Temple; now it is customary to bring flowers and plants to the synagogue.

Tishah B'Av (*Mourning for the Temple in Jerusalem*) This festival is a day of mourning for the Temple in Jerusalem destroyed by the Romans in the first century AD. All that remains of the Temple is one wall called the Wailing Wall because here devout Orthodox Jews mourn the Temple's destruction. Liberal Jews have ceased to pray for the Temple's restoration.

LIBERAL JUDAISM

Liberal Judaism guards strictly what it considers to be the lasting, most important aspect of the Law of the Torah and Talmud, but it has abandoned many of the rituals and observances of Orthodox Judaism, and brought organs, music and singing into the liberal synagogues.

Liberal Jews believe that life is precious and should be preserved. Therefore they will cooperate with any measures designed to alleviate suffering and preserve life (as too will Orthodox Jews with a very few exceptions).

Religious observances and articles

A patient may request Jewish prayer books and a copy of the Old Testament. He may bring a prayer shawl and a skullcap with him. The Sabbath is the Jewish holy day, beginning at sunset on Friday and finishing at sunset on Saturday.

Minister of religion

Nurses should contact the local Liberal Jewish rabbi (see local telephone directory), or in case of difficulty, the Union of Liberal and Progressive Synagogues in London (see Central London yellow pages).

Attitudes to aspects of care

So far as clothing is concerned Liberal Jews hold no strong views, although some men may wish to pray with their heads covered. There are no taboos about the body or hair, only a desire for privacy and modesty.

The patient requires a strictly vegetarian diet if a kosher diet is not available. Meat must be kosher, which means it should have been slaughtered by a specially trained butcher called a *shochet* who has killed the animal in a humane way according to religious law; as much of the blood as possible is drained from the meat. Meat from the pig, such as pork, ham, sausages, and bacon, is forbidden, also shellfish. Many Liberal Jews do not observe the dietary laws, as each individual treats diet as a matter of conscience.

There are no special requirements affecting drugs, alcohol or pain.

Treatment

Consent to treatment is the same as under British law. Liberal Jews are in favour of spare part and transplant surgery, and blood transfusion is also acceptable.

Family planning is encouraged but Liberal Jews believe that termination of pregnancy is a matter for the mother. On balance, however, it is likely that most Liberal Jews would oppose it, unless there is real mental or physical danger to the mother.

Terminal care, last offices and burial

Liberal Jews concentrate more on what the person has done in this life and less on the afterlife. Emphasis is placed on the good that a person has achieved and the good he will leave behind when he dies. There are no formal last rites. Prayers for the dying may be said by the rabbi or by family and friends. Liberal Jews prefer burial to cremation.

Relationships with others

The family plays a very special role in Judaism. In Liberal Judaism both men and women can sit together in the synagogue. There are also female rabbis, and Liberal Jews are tolerant of other religions.

Further reading

J. D. Rayner and B. Hooker, *Judaism for Today*, Union of Liberal and Progressive Synagogues, London, 1978.

ORTHODOX JUDAISM

Orthodox Jews follow very strictly the Jewish law as laid down in the Torah and Talmud.

Religious observances and articles

The Sabbath   The Sabbath starts at sunset on Friday and finishes when the stars appear in the sky on Saturday evening. It is strictly observed by all Orthodox or traditional Jews. All food for the Sabbath is prepared on Friday before sunset because no-one can do any work on the Sabbath — cook, switch on electrical appliances, drive, handle money or even write. The meal on Friday evening is the most important one of the week, and the father (or head of the house) blesses the bread and wine. The Sabbath itself is spent at synagogue, at home with the family and in quiet reflection and study. Sabbath ends with the lighting of a candle and a blessing is given for the coming week.

Circumcision   All male infants must be circumcized on the eighth day after birth. This ritual is usually attended by male members of the family and the circumcision is performed by a *mohel*, (a trained and registered circumcizer). Women members of the family may attend the ceremony if they wish.

Religious articles

The Orthodox Jewish male wears a skullcap (*yarmulke*) or other covering on his head and a prayer shawl (*tallith*) round his neck when praying. Many Jewish women wear a scarf on their heads. The patient may request a Jewish prayer book called a *siddor*. Male patients may also put on 'phylacteries' (small leather boxes containing prayers) in the morning.

Minister of religion

The nurse should call the local rabbi from the Orthodox Jewish synagogue. If in doubt she should telephone the office of the Chief Rabbi
in London (see Central London yellow pages).

Attitudes to aspects of care

Clothing   There is a group of extremely Orthodox Jews who wear very
distinctive clothing, which can be seen in Figure 1, page 23. Other
articles of clothing are mentioned above in the paragraph on religious
articles.

The body   The Orthodox Jew does not shave the face but some overcome the difficulty of having a full beard by using an electric razor.
This is relevant preoperatively as many anaesthetists prefer the patient
to be cleanshaven, and shaving off as much as is permitted normally
overcomes this difficulty. Many Jewish men and women prefer to keep
their heads covered at all times, often by a skullcap for the men and a
scarf for the women.

Both male and female Jewish patients prefer privacy and modesty,
although they do not mind being examined by doctors of either sex.
The body and life itself is believed by Jews to be a gift from God and
therefore it must not be abused by drugs, alcohol or other excesses.
Alcohol may be taken in moderation and drugs can be used if they are
for strictly medicinal purposes. Particular care should be taken to
ensure that drugs do not derive from the body of a pig, such as porcine
insulin, or from other forbidden food. Many patients adhere to these
dietary laws quite strictly, although permission may be given if, by
using such a drug or graft, life can be saved.

Diet   This is a very important aspect of caring for an Orthodox Jew.
The patient may ask to wash his hands and say a blessing before he
eats; he requires a kosher diet (see page 84), eating nothing that comes
in any way from a pig or other forbidden animals. He may be so strict
that he does not eat jelly because it could be made with gelatine from
a non-kosher animal, or some cheeses if any of the rennet comes from
a non-kosher animal. He does not eat shellfish nor any fish without fins
and scales.

An Orthodox Jew may not have meat and milk at the same meal;
three hours must elapse before milk can be taken after meat.

Utensils and crockery   Crockery and cutlery must also be washed up
separately. Meat dishes and cutlery may not be washed up with those
used for milk, and utensils and crockery from non-kosher meals must
not be washed up with crockery from a kosher meal. In a large hospi-

tal this creates problems, but some hospitals have overcome these by having a private arrangement with local Jewish caterers.* If this is not possible the patient may accept a vegetarian diet, or alternatively he may prefer his family to bring in kosher food on disposable plates.

Treatment

The Orthodox Jew has respect for the doctor and has no problems with consent to treatment, with one exception. He does not accept drugs, grafts or transplants that come from a pig or other forbidden animal, unless they are to save life, feeling it is wrong to refuse any treatment the doctor prescribes in order to save life.

Blood transfusions are quite permissible. Mechanical methods of contraception are not permitted but Jews almost invariably practise some form of contraception. They are very unlikely to condone termination of pregnancy unless it would be injurious to the health of the mother to do otherwise.

Terminal care, last offices and burial

The rabbi and/or a member of the family should be at the patient's bedside to recite prayers. The patient may wish to say a form of confession and, finally, he will be encouraged to say the Sh'ma Yisrael, a verse from *Deuteronomy*, 'Hear, O Israel the Lord our God, The Lord is one'. This is the first verse that an Orthodox Jewish child is taught and should be the last words on his lips when he dies.

When carrying out last offices the nurse can do very little, apart from closing the eyes, straightening the arms and hands and placing them by the sides of the patient's body. The jaws are then bandaged, and if permissible all tubes are removed with other attached equipment. The body is then wrapped in a plain sheet, and without any further interference placed in the mortuary or another room set aside for Jewish patients.

Traditionally a member of the synagogue and/or the family remains with the body, but this is normally waived in very large hospitals as someone is always in attendance. It is thought disrespectful by the Jews to leave a body unattended.

The body must be washed by officials from the local Jewish burial society specially trained in this rite, which is called the Tahara rite. It is a very important Jewish religious duty.

The body is regarded by the Jews as God's gift, therefore it should not be harmed or mutilated. Orthodox Jews may donate organs but only if by doing so they can preserve the life of someone else, and this may include medical research. They do not authorize a post-mortem examination of the body unless there is a legal requirement for it.

* The Hospital Kosher Meals Service provides kosher meals for all London hospitals.

Jews must be buried and not cremated, preferably in a Jewish cemetery.

Further reading

I. Jakobovits, *Jewish Medical Ethics*, Bloch, New York, 1959.

Sikhism

Sikhism is found in India, East Africa, Britain, Singapore and Hong Kong. It developed in India at the end of the fifteenth century, and its founder was Guru Nanak. Sikhism includes much of the teaching which is common to Muslims and Hindus.

Basic beliefs

Unlike Hindus, but like Muslims, Sikhs are completely monotheistic. But like Hindus, and unlike Muslims, they believe in reincarnation. One can find many of the ingredients of both these great religions in Sikhism, but it should be seen as a completely independent and unique religion.

Sikhism is based on the teaching of ten gurus. The last of these, Guru Govind Singh died in 1708 and he decreed that there would be no further gurus but that the teachings of the gurus should be considered holy. These teachings can be found in *Adi-Granth* (or *Granth Sahib*), the revered holy book of the Sikhs.

Sikhs believe in one God, transmigration of the soul, reincarnation and a strict code of discipline, in which Sikhs must help others, and be truthful, generous and kind. They must be loyal to God and to the community. They must rise early, say prayers at sunrise, sunset and before going to bed. They must not commit adultery and must give one-tenth of their income to the local *gurdwara* (Sikh temple) or to local charity.

A Sikh must be baptized according to the rites of the Sikh religion and must be able to read and write Punjabi. He must be ready to defend his religion and people at all times, hence the rule about always carrying a weapon (now usually symbolic) and the strict emphasis on physical fitness.

The local *gurdwara* is more than just a religious place of worship, but is also a community centre for all Sikhs in the neighbourhood.

Religious observances and articles

Patient may like to have booklets of the Sikh holy scriptures and a visit from one of the leaders of the local Sikh community. Other articles are described under aspects of care below as they are relevant to the physical care of the patient.

Minister of religion

The nurse should contact the nearest *gurdwara* and ask one of its leaders to come and see the patient, or arrange for him to be visited. Strictly speaking there are no priests in Sikhism but there are holy men, and local Sikh leaders often use the term 'priest' so they can be more easily identified.

Attitudes to aspects of care

Even though much of it is now symbolic, Sikh men dress in a way that is in keeping with the duty to be ready at all times to defend themselves. Sikhs have to wear a number of objects on them which have great religious significance, and when undressing an unconscious male Sikh patient, nurses should keep as many of these objects on the patient as it is safe to do.

The five principal religious symbols are easy to remember as they all begin with the letter K and are referred to as the 5 Ks. They are:
Kes, uncut hair
Kangha, the comb
Kara, a steel bangle
Kirpan, a dagger
Kacha, white shorts

Kes, uncut hair None of a Sikh's hair may be cut, including hair on the head, face and body. Local Sikh leaders may give permission for hair to be removed in an emergency, so long as it is absolutely essential and a bare minimum is removed.

Kangha, the comb This is a small comb worn in the hair which is then covered by a turban.

Kara, a steel bangle Sikhs must wear a steel bangle on their wrists.

Kirpan, a dagger As British law is very strict on the wearing and carrying of knives and other sharp-pointed weapons, some Sikhs wear a small symbolic dagger, but many also wear throwing rings in their turbans.

Kacha, white shorts These are worn as underwear by Sikh men, who should be allowed to wear them in hospital if at all possible.

There are few dress requirements for Sikh women. The majority wear a sari or other long dress and all keep their heads covered with a scarf. Female patients may be reluctant or may actually refuse to undress in front of a male nurse or doctor, the majority preferring to be examined by a female doctor.

Some Sikhs accept anything to eat, but many prefer not to eat beef in any form, such as steak, stews, soups, beef extracts, sausages and pies; some may even be completely vegetarian.

There are no restrictions on drugs and alcohol, but they must be taken in moderation and some Sikhs refuse both unless they are medically absolutely necessary. Sikhs do not smoke at all.

Treatment

There are no requirements for consent to treatment other than those required by law. Spare part and transplant surgery are permissible and so are blood transfusions. Termination of pregnancy and contraception are left for each family to decide.

Terminal care, last offices and burial

A dying Sikh will appreciate passages from the holy book *Adi-Granth* being read to him by a leader from the local *gurdwara*. He will also welcome the company of his family or members of the local Sikh community. There are no particular last offices. On the whole Sikhs have no objection to post-mortem examinations but it is wise to treat each family individually. Sikhs are always cremated, not buried.

Shinto

Shinto is an ancient religion still found in Japan and among many Japanese people throughout the world. It is a national religion without scriptures.

Basic beliefs

Those who embrace the Shinto religion believe in a vast number of gods and goddesses. Shinto itself means the 'Way of the Gods'. For example, there are gods of the sea, the sky, the earth and the home. The chief goddess is Amaterasu, and legend has it that the first Emperor of Japan was a descendant of Amaterasu and is therefore himself divine.

As a result there is an emphasis on ancestor worship and on worship in the countryside, though there is no public worship for followers of Shinto. Individuals pray at one of the hundreds of small shrines scattered all over Japan, the most famous temple to Amaterasu being at Ise in Japan. Priests also pray at the shrines but most Shinto priests have other employment too. Buddhism and Shinto had a great influence upon each other, especially where Zen Buddhism is concerned (see page 52). While Shinto is still to be found in Japan it does not appear to have quite the same following as Buddhism.

There are a few nursing points to be made. Respect must be given to the reverence afforded to a patient's body by a bereaved family. Nurses should also be aware of a group within Shinto called the Tenri-Kyo who practice faith healing.

If the patient turns towards the rising sun in the morning bows and claps his hands he is usually giving thanks to Amaterasu and hoping that he will be blessed with a good day ahead.

Taoism

As an organized religion Taoism is virtually dead, but like Confucianism it still has an influence on Chinese thought and culture, and concepts of social behaviour. The Chinese attitude to authority, social status, work and personal development are also rooted in Taoism and Confucianism, and also expresses itself in their art and folk lore. The gaiety and happiness found in the celebration of the Chinese New Year in London, San Francisco and Hong Kong for instance, demonstrate some of the traditions of Taoism.

Basic beliefs

The most important book in Taoism is the *Tao-Te-Ching*. Taoism stems from *Tao* meaning the Way, which is more than just a way of life to follow and includes the Way of Heaven, the Way of Earth, the Way of Nature and so on. It is a concept of peace and harmony which finds itself in all that is natural and peaceful.

Taoism includes the concept of Yang and Yin. Yang is heaven which is perceived to be full of sunlight and is predominantly masculine. Yin, on the other hand, represents the earth which is dark and feminine. Harmony exists when the Yin and Yang are well-balanced, and this not only makes for harmony in individuals but in the universe as a whole. Taoism has influenced Buddhism and vice versa, and becomes inextricably combined with Confucianism, especially in its cultural manifestations.

Religious movements which have their foundation in Christianity

The following religious movements which grew out of Christianity need to be discussed individually. They are:
The Church of Jesus Christ of Latter Day Saints (Mormons)
The Church of Christ, Scientist
The Church of God
The Jehovah's Witnesses
The Spiritualist Association of Great Britain
The Unitarian Church

THE CHURCH OF JESUS CHRIST OF LATTER DAY SAINTS (MORMONS)

The members of this group are most commonly referred to as 'Mormons' because they follow the teachings of the Book of Mormon. The Church of Jesus Christ of Latter Day Saints was founded by the prophet Joseph Smith, Jr. in the United States. He was told in a vision where to find ancient gold plates which were written in reformed Egyptian; these Mormons believe were given to Joseph Smith from God together with the power to translate these works. The Book of Mormon is the translation of this scripture.

Joseph Smith's successor was Brigham Young who continued to spread this new message, which attracted many followers. They were persecuted and moved across America to the Great Salt Lake in Utah where they founded Salt Lake City which has been the home of the Church of Jesus Christ of Latter Day Saints ever since. Their churches are to be found in almost every country that is free from religious oppression or governmental restrictions on religion.

Basic beliefs

Mormons believe in God and in the divinity of Jesus Christ. They also believe the Book of Mormon to be scripture in addition to the Bible. The Book of Mormon tells of a remnant group of the House of Israel who in the sixth century BC was led to the Americas, and descendants of whom are the American Indians. After wars among the peoples, only Moroni, the son of Mormon, was left, and it was he who visited Joseph Smith to give him the records hidden in the side of the hill Cumorah, from which he translated the Book of Mormon. The latter also tells of Jesus Christ visiting the Americas after his ascension. Mormons also have a strong belief in the power of the resurrection, and in life after death.

Religious observances and articles

The patient usually wishes to pray twice daily, morning and evening and should be allowed the necessary privacy to do so. He may request the Holy Bible (King James edition), the Book of Mormon, the Doctrine and Covenants and a book called the *Pearl of Great Price*.

Minister of religion

The local lay minister of the Church of Jesus Christ of Latter Day Saints is known as a Bishop or a Branch President (depending on the size of the local community). He can be contacted through the local church most evenings and on Sundays (see the local yellow pages).

Attitudes to aspects of care

Clothing   A large number of members of the Church of Jesus Christ of Latter Day Saints wear clothing of a specific and sacred religious significance. The garment is considered to be *very* sacred by members of the Church and should be treated with great deference. The garment is worn in place of the usual underclothing underneath one's normal clothing, and consists of a white one or two-piece garment which covers the upper and lower body. A person in full control of their mental and/or physical faculties should be allowed to wear the garment while in hospital until such time as it becomes obstructive to medical or nursing treatment or care, when it may be removed. If the person is capable of removing the garment by himself he should be allowed to do so. In case of emergency, incapacity or death where the patient cannot remove the garment himself, a nurse or doctor may do so, but very respectfully. If there is any problem contact the local Bishop.

Members of the Church of Jesus Christ of Latter Day Saints also believe in spiritual healing, and may ask for a visit by a local church leader for a 'blessing' either on admittance to hospital in an emergency or before an operation.

Diet   They abstain from drinking tea, coffee, alcohol, and cola drinks, and they also refrain from smoking. They are required to fast once every month for 24 hours, but this can be waived while undergoing medical care unless the doctor believes that continuation of the fast will cause the patient no harm. Any prescribed drug may be taken.

Treatment

There are no special religious laws regarding consent to treatment. The Church of Jesus Christ of Latter Day Saints leaves all questions of spare part or transplant surgery to the conscience of the individual, provided it is carried out with dignity and respect for the family's wishes.

It also opposes the termination of pregnancy although, after counsel and prayer, consideration may be given to cases of termination where the mother is the victim of rape or where her life is in danger. Family planning and sterilization is also for the conscience of the individual to decide upon should these be necessary, for instance where failure to do so could result in harm to the mother. Blood transfusions are permissible.

Terminal care, last offices and burial

The Church of Jesus Christ of Latter Day Saints hold life to be sacred and, while they are totally opposed to euthanasia, they believe that the dying should be made comfortable, treated with dignity and kept free from pain. There are no last rites and, in the absence of a minister of their own religion, they do not welcome the rites of another sect or religion or, for example, to be seen by the hospital chaplain.

THE CHURCH OF CHRIST, SCIENTIST (CHRISTIAN SCIENTISTS)

The Church of Christ, Scientist, was founded in 1879 in Boston, Massachusetts by Mrs Mary Baker Eddy. It is found in 57 countries of the world especially in North America and western Europe.

Basic beliefs

Christian Scientists believe that disease in all its forms can be healed by prayer alone. They regard the healings of Jesus Christ and of the early church as the outcome of the understanding of spiritual law that is available in every age.

Religious observances and articles

Church services are held on Sundays and Wednesday evenings. Each church maintains a Reading Room, where Christain Science literature may be read or obtained. The patient is likely to want a copy of the Holy Bible and the Christian Science textbook, *Science and Health with Key to the Scriptures* by Mary Baker Eddy.

He may also wish to have treatment through prayer from a Christian Science practitioner, if one is available, engaged in the church's healing ministry. Practitioners are listed in the *Christian Science Journal*, the official organ of the Church. To obtain a copy of the *Journal* and for further help, contact a Reading Room.

Attitudes to aspects of care

There are no special attitudes to clothing, diet, body and hair. Christian Scientists normally rely on prayer for healing, but some may accept analgesics for strong pain.

Treatment

There are no difficulties about consent to treatment. If Christian Scientists accept conventional treatment, they do so under the normal legal conditions which apply in the United Kingdom. Christian Scientists relying upon prayer for healing do not take drugs. They take their children to doctors in accordance with child care legislation, and submit them to the treatment prescribed. Immunization and quarantine regulations are observed, but spare part and transplant surgery is not normally accepted. Termination of pregnancy is permitted in exceptional lifesaving circumstances. Family planning is a matter for the individual, but the Christian Scientist does not generally use the contraceptive pill considering it a drug. They allow broken bones to be set.

Terminal care, last offices and burial

There are no special aspects to the care of the terminally ill Christian Scientist, except that he will probably wish to have a fellow Christian Scientist to support him and his family.

Further reading

The Christian Science Publishing Society, *Questions and Answers on Christian Science*, Boston, Mass., 1974.

The Christian Science Publishing Society, *A Century of Christian Science Healing*, Boston, Mass., 1966.

THE CHURCH OF GOD

The Church of God is found in Africa, the Caribbean, the United Kingdom and the United States.

Basic beliefs

The beliefs of the Church of God are based on the Holy Bible and especially on the ten commandments. Its adherents also believe in baptism by total immersion.

Religious observances and articles

The patient may request a copy of the Holy Bible and a hymn book.

Minister of religion

The local minister from the Church of God should see the patient.

Attitudes to aspects of care

Members of the Church of God must be modestly dressed but otherwise there are no particular attitudes to the body or hair. Members of this sect cannot eat food containing blood products, such as black pudding. Many prefer herbal medicines to the conventional variety, and they must refrain from drinking alcohol. There are no special attitudes to pain and its relief.

Treatment

There are no restrictions concerning consent to treatment, spare part or transplant surgery. The Church of God opposes termination of pregnancy except when absolutely essential on medical but not on social grounds.

Terminal care, last offices and burial

There are no special rites or last offices. The patient should be seen by the Church of God minister.

JEHOVAH'S WITNESSES

Jehovah's Witnesses have their modern roots in America dating back to the end of the last century, and it is now a worldwide religion. The group began with missionary zeal to produce tracts published by what is now the Watch Tower Bible and Tract Society.

Basic beliefs

To Jehovah's Witnesses, the Holy Bible is inspired scripture which must be heeded. They hold some beliefs in common with other Christian groups but they differ in their faith in the following way: they believe that God will destroy the present world order at Armageddon; that only laws that do not conflict with God's laws should be obeyed; that the wicked will be eternally destroyed; that only a flock of 144 000 will go to heaven; that the earth will be inhabited as a paradise; that Satan is the invisible ruler of the world; that a clergy and special titles are improper; that man did not evolve but was created; and that taking blood into the body through the mouth or veins is a violation of God's laws.

Religious observances and articles

The patient may request a copy of the Holy Bible if he does not have one.

Minister of religion

The nurse should contact the local congregation elders. All Witnesses now carry a Medical Alert card giving all necessary emergency medical information and a contact address.

Attitudes to aspects of care

There are no special needs where clothing, body, hair, and diet are concerned. The patient may take prescribed drugs, including analgesia, on a doctor's advice and in accordance with his own convictions. He may drink alcohol if this does not trouble his conscience. An area free of tobacco smoke will be appreciated as Jehovah's Witnesses do not use tobacco.

Treatment

Jehovah's Witnesses have no restrictions on consent to treatment except in the case of blood transfusion which they will not accept for themselves nor for their next of kin and children. This also includes human plasma. This causes problems for doctor and patient alike when contemplating surgery, especially major surgery if the surgeon wishes to give a blood transfusion, and for spare part and transplant surgery a considerable amount may be required. Whether to undergo such surgery is for the individual to decide.

There are, however, new developments such as perfluorochemicals currently being researched, that can make life a little easier for the patient and doctor alike since Jehovah's Witnesses may be able to accept them along with existing non-blood volume expanders such as Dextran, Haemadel and ordinary electrolyte infusions such as Ringer's lactate (Hartmann's Solution).

This delicate problem of blood transfusion can create an ethical dilemma for the doctor and possibly the patient's family. Most doctors now seek an alternative form of treatment such as a diet rich in iron and the use of non-blood volume expanders during surgery, often accompanied by intramuscular injections of iron. These produce successful results in many cases, and Jehovah's Witnesses appreciate this care.

The most sensitive and controversial issue arises when the patient is a child. In some cases doctors have asked for legal help and intervention to make the child a ward of court. But this course of action should be avoided whenever possible. If, however, it should occur the hospital solicitor should be notified; but many people find this an infringement of the parents' rights to bring a child up to follow their religion. What, however, is the doctor to do if the child is suffering from leukaemia and requires a blood transfusion to replace the immature and neoplastic cells? Or if indeed the child needs a bone marrow transplant? This is not only a difficult dilemma for a Jehovah's Witness and for the doctor, but it also raises some fundamental questions for society.

Jehovah's Witnesses hold strong views on the termination of pregnancy and are totally opposed to it with the possible exception of an ectopic pregnancy. But they are not opposed to contraception which they regard as being a matter for the couple to decide.

Terminal care, last offices and burial

Jehovah's Witnesses do not support euthanasia but they believe that if death is imminent and unavoidable, life should not be prolonged artificially. There are no last rites for Jehovah's Witnesses but they appreciate the support and prayers of fellow Witnesses. They believe that the human soul ceases to exist at death but that the resurrection of the dead to life on earth will come one day.

Relationships with others

Jehovah's Witnesses believe that their's is the only correct religion, and they therefore feel unable to play any part in interfaith movements.

Further reading

Watch Tower Bible and Tract Society, *Jehovah's Witnesses in the Twentieth Century*, 1979.

Watchtower Bible and Tract Society, *Jehovah's Witnesses and the Question of Blood*, 1977.

THE SPIRITUALIST ASSOCIATION OF GREAT BRITAIN

Basic beliefs

Spiritualists believe that the soul survives bodily death and under certain conditions can communicate with loved ones on earth.

Religious observances and articles

There are no special spiritualist observances or articles but some patients may request a copy of the Holy Bible or other religious book.

Minister of religion

If the patient requires help and support he may ask to see the local spiritualist minister (see the local yellow pages).

Attitudes to aspects of care

With regard to clothing, body and hair there are no particularly different attitudes. Some Spiritualists are vegetarians but otherwise they have no dietary regulations. They may take alcohol, but in moderation, and while they can take drugs including analgesia for medical reasons they regard suffering as a necessity in life.

Attitudes to treatment

Spiritualists have no objection to spare part or transplant surgery, blood transfusion, family planning or termination of pregnancy — provided that the latter is performed only in order to save the life of the mother.

Terminal care, last offices and burial

There are no particular last offices, but the patient may appreciate a visit from the local Spiritualist minister. Some Spiritualists have an intense dislike of cremation.

THE UNITARIANS

The Unitarian Movement began in Europe, having its roots in the Protestant Reformation. It has many strands. The oldest existing organization of churches is in Hungary and Rumania, dating from 1568. Most of the oldest English congregations grew out of the ejection of Puritans from the Church of England in 1662. Scottish and Welsh Unitarianism have different origins, and in Ireland, Unitarians belong to the Non-Subscribing Presbyterian Church of Ireland. There are also Unitarians in the Commonwealth, Czechoslovakia, Denmark, South Africa, the United States and West Germany.

Basic beliefs

Unitarianism has no fixed creed and no doctrinal test for membership or the ministry. Unitarian ministers seek to persuade and not dictate. Unitarians consist of a mixture of persuasions varying from Liberal Christian to religious humanist and there are also universalists among Unitarians who seek to know something of the truth in all major religions.

Some Unitarians regard Unitarianism as a religion in its own right and not as a denomination of Christianity. However there are some general

Christian attitudes in the Unitarian Church. For example, although most Unitarians do not believe the doctrine of the Holy Trinity, many aver that they know of no better man in religious history than Jesus of Nazareth, but they believe that there were also other good men in the past and that there may be others like him in the future. However, this must also be seen within the Unitarians' liberal approach to religious belief which they consider does not necessarily lie in the Bible or in the Church but within the individual. The Unitarian movement has female ministers.

Religious observances and articles

Most Unitarian patients would appreciate a quiet time for reflection and prayer. They may request some religious texts, but do not usually expect sacraments (except perhaps in Ireland).

Minister of religion

The nurse should contact the local Unitarian minister (see the local telephone directory), or if this proves difficult the London Headquarters of the Unitarian General Assembly (see Central London yellow pages). Some Unitarians may be equally pleased to see any of the hospital chaplains or, if at home, a local minister of religion from any denomination.

Attitudes to aspects of care

The attitudes of Unitarians to clothing the body, hair, pain and drugs are no different from those which prevail in Britain. Some Unitarians abstain totally from alcohol and some are vegetarian.

Treatment

Unitarians have no restrictions on consent to treatment, spare part and transplant surgery or blood transfusion, or family planning. They mostly consider termination of pregnancy to be a matter for a joint decision by the parents.

Terminal care, last offices and burial

There are no special rites or last offices, but naturally many Unitarians and their families wish to see their Unitarian minister. Most Unitarians prefer cremation.

Relationships with others

In general Unitarians respect the religions and cultures of others but they do not agree with those which diminish and restrict human freedom.

Further reading

A. Hill, *What Unitarians Believe*, Lindsey Press, 1973.

RASTAFARIANISM

Rastafarianism can be found in Ethopia, Jamaica and in the United Kingdom. Rastafarianism was founded when Ras Tafari became the Emperor of Ethiopia in 1930. He was known as Haile Selassie and also called himself 'King of Kings' and the 'Lion of Judah'. Those who had previously followed a negro leader called Marcus Garvey believed that Haile Selassie was the Messiah. Rastafarianism has a great following among young Jamaicans, other West Indians and those who are descended from Jamaican families. There are very few white people in the movement.

Basic beliefs

Rastafarians believe, as stated above, that Haile Selassie is God and that he will lead black people to salvation in Ethiopia which is heaven to Rastafarians. They believe that they are descended from the tribes of Israel and that they are in exile as a result of the behaviour of the white man.

Religious observances and articles

A Rastafarian patient may ask for a copy of the Holy Bible. He may also bring with him a copy of the Ethiopian Orthodox Bible. He may wish to seek the advice and support of one of the local Rastafarian leaders, but if this proves difficult, the headquarters of the movement should be contacted (through the London telephone directory).

One of the Rastafarian symbols is the Lion which represents the Lion of Judah, the late Emperor Haile Selassie. Much of the flavour of and the message of Rastafarianism can be found in the reggae music of Bob Marley (who died recently). Some Rastafarians may be under the influence of a form of cannabis which they call *ganja* or 'the herb' and which they use for the purpose of meditation. This drug is illegal in Britain so few patients will admit to taking it.

Attitudes to aspects of care

Rastafarians wear clothing made of natural fibres, such as wool, silk and cotton, avoiding synthetic materials. Most Rastafarian women wear woollen socks rather than tights or nylon stockings; they are forbidden to wear trousers and must keep their heads covered usually with a scarf.

Most Rastafarians are vegetarians but some eat any meat except pork. They may not eat anything from the vine, such as currants or grapes. Exceptionally strict Rastafarians will only eat food cooked in vegetable oil and do not eat in public. Strict Rastafarians may refuse all drugs except *ganja*, and the majority only use drugs prescribed for medical reasons.

They have no particular taboos about their bodies but their hair plays a very important part in their religion. They must not cut it and strictly speaking should not comb it either — this uncut hair is referred to as 'dreadlocks'. Shaving prior to surgery may be accepted reluctantly but the patient may be very unwilling to have his hair washed unless he can be convinced that it is absolutely essential.

Treatment

Rastafarians accept all treatment except spare part and transplant surgery, and they will not undergo termination of pregnancy. Many Rastafarians refuse blood transfusions but this is an entirely individual matter. The only forms of contraception acceptable to Rastafarians are the sheath and the rhythm method.

Terminal care and last offices and burial

There are no special offices but the patient may ask a fellow Rastafarian to support him by reading prayers.

Further reading

E. D. Barrett, *The Rastafarians — The Dreadlocks of Jamaica*, Heinemann, London, 1977.

E. D. Cronon, *Black Moses*, University of Wisconsin Press, 1969.

T. Nicholas, *Rastafari — A Way of Life*, Doubleday Anchor Original, 1979.

5. THE TEACHING OF MEDICAL AND NURSING ETHICS

General

The teaching of medical and nursing ethics has been a subject for lively debate, especially in the *Journal of Medical Ethics*. Can such codes of practice be usefully discussed, hypothetically, in the classroom? Can they be properly learned only on the wards by the teaching and example of skilled experienced and respected practitioners, or is there a time and place for both? The notion that ethics can be taught *only* in the classroom is, fortunately, almost extinct and is a relic of the days when ethics, etiquette and legal considerations were hopelessly muddled together. There are very few nurse-teachers still around who adhere to this way of teaching ethics, but many will remember lectures on ethics which concentrated on the proper way to address a consultant! Thus their main surviving effect on the teaching of ethics is that so many of their students rebelled that the pendulum has perhaps swung far in the other direction and has led to the belief that ethics can and should be taught only through practical experience.

The two main alternatives

Opinion now seems to be divided between those who think that ethics can be taught only by clinical practice, and those who acknowledge the supremacy of hard experience, but believe that thoughtfully prepared classroom teaching along the lines of introductory talks, discussion and role-play can also make a contribution. Although the first point of view is to be respected it does not appear to go far enough, in view of the multiple nature of ethical dilemmas in medicine and nursing. Experience alone does not always present a comprehensive curriculum. It can be one-sided, emotional and prejudiced — as indeed can any single-minded training method. Ethical complexities have become too important and pervasive to be relegated to one form of teaching only. A more balanced approach is now required.

Experience alone does not acquaint the student with all the possible outcomes of a problem, and she may be forced by circumstances to act beyond her competence long before her training is completed, let alone before she has acquired enough experience to develop her judgement properly. Also, young teenage students already have strong but generally badly informed prejudices which, if left unchallenged at an early stage, will become set in concrete long before they can be influenced by experience. Classroom or 'off the ward' teaching helps to bring an element of preparation, emotional detachment and balance to the subject. It has been tried and it works!

The value of classroom discussion

Take as an example, an actual discussion with first-year student nurses on the ethical problems of artificially terminating pregnancy. At the beginning, the class could not understand the need to discuss the matter at all. Most of them already had a fixed prejudice that abortion was either all right or all wrong! It was either every woman's self-evident right, or evil murder. A few other possibilities were thrown in for reflection and discussion, such as the birth of a badly deformed baby, the possible death of the mother, the plight of the rape victim and so on. After a lively debate, most of those who had begun with such confident prejudice had become less black and white in their reactions and more open to later clinical teaching on the wards. The seeds of reason had been planted to grow and do continuing battle with prejudice and emotion.

Such discussions at the early student stage stimulate an awareness of the ethical dimension which may not have existed before and provoke the curiosity and spirit of enquiry that lie at the roots of all good teaching. For example, the same discussion mentioned above went on to consider the emotional difficulties the students had already encountered, or which they imagined would present themselves, in a gynaecological ward where patients under investigation for infertility were placed alongside those having pregnancies terminated.

Training for handling emergencies

Some ethical judgements have to be made instantly, as in deciding whether or not to resuscitate. This provides an example of how classroom discussion can merge into ward-based teaching and experience. The possibility that a patient may collapse should first be raised in the classroom, perhaps in a discussion on medical and nursing ethics, or after a demonstration on resuscitation techniques. Unless students are introduced to the idea that occasionally it can be inhumane to resuscitate (a point that may not have occurred to them), one may find that students and practitioners *will always* resuscitate without ever thinking or discussing the matter with the consultant and his team before, say, a terminally ill patient actually collapses during the night. Such previous discussion may well prevent agonized decision-making at the time, the infliction of unnecessarily prolonged suffering on the patient, criticism of the nurse and her subsequent collapse of confidence. This is not to say that every, or even most, such crises can be foreseen — merely that tragedies *can* be prevented by proper and imaginative training, both in the classroom and on the wards. The two are complementary, the first being an important preparation for the second.

Training methods

In classroom teaching, however, the methods used are all-important. An introduction to the ethical perspective in medicine and nursing is an essential preliminary by lecture or seminar. This identifies the subject and distinguishes it from law and etiquette, which should be treated separately. Regular discussion and role-play on the important moral dilemmas should then follow first in the classroom and later in the wards, departments and health centres, and can be reinforced by essays and projects. No opportunity should be lost to bring the ethical dimension into all aspects of clinical teaching, where appropriate, as it is only in this way that the proper consideration of both clinical and ethical factors can be effectively combined at the earliest possible stage in the development of mature and experienced judgement.

Cultural and religious variations

So far, the consideration has been generally of training that is deemed appropriate to *all* medical and nursing ethics, whether in the field of ethical norms or cultural and religious variations. The practical dangers of defining too closely, especially in writing, the limits to be set on clinical actions and procedures should be re-emphasized. But where cultural and religious variations are concerned, the volume of unfamiliar detail that needs to be absorbed, outside the ethical norms with which nurse and doctor should be familiar, must be developed in textbook form both as a teaching aid and as a work of reference. Discussion and role-play in the classroom can be developed from the material presented in it.

ADDING THE CULTURAL AND RELIGIOUS DIMENSIONS

The first thing to be said is that no attempt should be made to add the cultural and religious dimensions until the student first has a grounding in the ethical norms although it should be remembered that, even here, there are important indigenous variations to be considered. We are, of course, already into an area that is complex and difficult enough in an intrinsically delicate subject. As in all aspects of training, we must bring students along as quickly as possible without overloading them too soon.

However, we cannot leave it too late either, or we could, for example, find an Irish Roman Catholic student nurse left to supervise the aborfacient intravenous infusion of a non-English speaking Muslim patient, who is being treated by a male, agnostic West Indian doctor in an English hospital!

Readers should by now comprehend at once the nuances involved. A female Muslim patient is likely to oppose abortion on religious grounds. It may not be apparent to her that this intravenous infusion will terminate her pregnancy, unless she is told. Her few words of English would not be a sufficient vehicle for the staff to convey this important information and the medical imperative behind it, nor for her to express her ethical objections to it. Even if she herself consented to this treatment, after all the circumstances had been properly explained to her (which might not be practicable in the case of a sudden emergency) she would be likely to incur the anger of her husband, at the very least, and possible ostracism by her family. In any case, she could find it abhorrent to be examined by a male doctor, who in this particular case might not accord much weight to her ethical objections in view of the clinical priorities. The Roman Catholic nurse, depending on the strength of her own conviction about her Church's attitude towards abortion, might find herself severely torn between her natural sympathy for the patient's ethical objection and the clinical judgement of the doctor. Her position as a student nurse may incline her to defer to the doctor's judgement, but may not dim her resentment if she considers that the outcome was morally wrong or if she feels that the patient's sensibilities were outraged, ignored or not handled sympathetically enough. Even if the patient *does* consent to treatment after the clinical factors and urgency have been properly explained to her she may, in this case, refuse to sign a consent form, expecting it to be a matter for her husband, father or brother since her culture does not accord her the right to make such decisions for herself.

Now, without any classroom teaching, this student nurse could find herself in a similar such position before she has had any introduction to the nuances involved. The example may sound complex and far-fetched, but is in fact a not impossible situation to find in a British hospital today. So, once the basic ethical norms have been addressed and the student has some grounding in the subject, an introductory lecture and some textbook reading could be inserted before the student is likely to become too closely involved with this kind of situation on the wards.

Discussion, role-play and teaching on the ward can follow, combined throughout with training in the more normal ethical codes of practice. Reinforcement by essays and projects can, for ethical variations, be supplemented by seminars, symposia, visits, and films. These can draw in ministers of religion, community relations councils, general practitioners and consultants, who either come from the minority groups in question themselves or have frequent dealings with them. Most hospital chaplains are willing to take part in discussions on ethics, and spiritual and terminal care. They also play an increasingly large part in counselling medical, nursing and other staff in the hospital.

Not all training need encroach on teaching hours, nor need it become a tedious addition to an already crowded curriculum. For example, the school can maintain a calendar of religious and social events on a multiracial and non-sectarian basis, which can lead students into enjoying such spectacles as a Chinese New Year in Soho or the Hindu festival of Holi. These occasions usually end with new friendships, which can remove a load from the shoulders of the nurse-teacher! An imaginative hospital can also involve its invariably multiethnic staff and students by helping them to organize, in turn, on one day a year for each group, some form of social activity for each ethnic tradition. These occasions can be enjoyable for all concerned, and are instructive for teachers, staff and students in all aspects of cultural and religious variations. It would also promote confidence between the hospital and the local catchment area.

The nursing process

The spiritual and cultural needs of the patient can easily be woven into the nursing process. A careful analysis of his needs can be made while taking a nursing history, in carrying out observations, and may be incorporated in the nursing care plan. The evaluation of the effectiveness of this care is more difficult to assess but it may be done by using a similar set of objectives as one would for assessing the alleviation of any other stress factors. The evaluation has to answer two basic questions: What was done? Did it work?

What was done?   Perhaps it was the provision of some religious article, arranging a visit from a friend or minister of religion, ordering the appropriate diet, or respecting the religious traditions of the patient during the final phase of his life.

Did it work?   In some instances this can be easy to evaluate, for example, when the patient is visited by his minister of religion and appears afterwards more relaxed and at ease with himself. Some cultural aspects of care may be less easy to evaluate but not impossible. Poor results could be due to failures in understanding and communication between the various members of the team.

Multidisciplinary training

The introduction (page 1) referred to the dangers that are looming beyond the horizons of scientific advance, and especially to the problems one can encounter if one does not face the outside world with a joint approach to ethical considerations. One way of formulating and preserving a joint approach would be by joint or multidisciplinary training. The case should not be overstated. Some areas of ethical judgement are becoming so technical as to be comprehensible only to the most eminent leaders in a particular field. But the frontiers of knowledge are covered by the two-tier interpretation developed in the introduction above, and concern matters which, while being common enough practice on the wards, are shared by doctors, nurses and others and are subject to ethical considerations.

Many ethical topics lend themselves to fruitful interdisciplinary discussion. This not only fosters a more broadminded and informed approach to ethical dilemmas but normally benefits doctors, nurses, and paramedical personnel (both students and practitioners) by giving them insights into each other's professions, into those difficulties that are unique to each, and common to all. One tends to emerge from these sessions with enhanced mutual confidence and greater respect for each other's profession. The spiritual and cultural care of patients is just one small important area which could be explored together.

It is here, in the author's opinion, that at least some training sessions along the lines previously described should be developed on an interdisciplinary basis. Perhaps the most serious real problem — as opposed to prejudice, habit and inertia — might be the practical difficulty of harmonizing the different training schedules involved, referred to above as an example of an administrative restraint upon the implementation of policy. However, those restraints can usually be overcome by determination, skill and ingenuity — if the end is considered important enough; and this must be judged by those who have responsibility for and the ordering of such matters. If universities can arrange their curricula to allow students to take courses in other faculties, then so can medicine and nursing schools. The real question is whether the importance of such a project is worth the administrative cost, and if so whether the motivation and determination to change existing practice can be aroused.

If anyone still denies the importance of the spiritual and cultural care of patients, then consider the future danger of lack of communication between indigenous doctors and nurses, or other practitioners and visiting or immigrant staff, which can lead to misunderstanding, differences in attitude and other serious problems. Such misunderstandings, of course, are not confined to those from other countries, creeds and cultures. Prejudices of all kinds arise in ethical dilemmas, and especially when national and racial prejudices are at work. Failures of communication arise from a wide variety of causes and the resulting misunderstandings can be experienced with and by indigenous group and newcomers alike, in both overt and subtle ways. An increased sensitivity toward the need for better understanding and increased communication can lead to a more harmonious and peaceful society.

SELECTED BIBLIOGRAPHY

C. Blomquist, R. M. Veatch, and D. Fenner, 'The teaching of medical ethics', *Journal of Medical Ethics*, vol. 1, no. 2, pp. 96–103, July 1975.

M. Bunzl, 'A note on nursing ethics in the USA', *Journal of Medical Ethics*, vol. 1, no. 4, p. 184, December 1975.

A. V. Campbell, *Moral Dilemmas in Medicine*, 2nd edn, Churchill Livingstone, Edinburgh, 1976.

A. L. Clark, *Culture, Childbearing, Health Professionals*, Davis, Philadelphia, 1978.

G. Cleverly, and B. Phillips, *Northbourne Tales of Belief and Understanding*, McGraw-Hill, Maidenhead, 1975.

Consumer's Association, *What To Do When Someone Dies*, 8th edn, 1977.

H. Faber, *Pastoral Care in the Modern Hospital*, SCM, London, 1971.

B. Gascoigne, *The Christians*, Jonathan Cape, London, 1979.

J. H. Gerstner, *The Theology of the Major Sects*, Baker, Grand Rapids, Michigan, 1960.

A. Hindley, 'Asian patients in hospital and at home,' King Edward's Hospital Fund, London, 1979.

R. Hughes, *Borrowed Time, Borrowed Place: Hong Kong and its Many Faces*, 2nd edn, Deutsch, London, 1976.

Lord Kilbrandon, P. D. Nuttall and Z. Butrym, 'Ethics and the professions', *Journal of Medical Ethics*, vol. 1, no. 1, pp. 2–4, 1975.

King Edward's Hospital Fund for London, 'The hospital chaplain: An enquiry into the role of the hospital chaplain', London, 1966.

J. Laffin, *The Dagger of Islam*, Sphere, London, 1979.

Lothian Community Relations Councils, 'Religions and cultures: A guide to patients' beliefs and customs for health service staff', Edinburgh, 1978.

U. Maclean, *Magical Medicine: A Nigerian Case Study*, Penguin, Harmondsworth, 1971.

C. Nakane, *Japanese Society*, Penguin, Harmondsworth, 1973.

W. Owen Cole (ed.), *World Religions: A Handbook for Teachers*, Commission for Racial Equality, London, 1977.

E. G. Parrinder, *Worship in the World's Religions*, Sheldon, London, 1961.

E. G. Parrinder, *A Book of World Religions*, Hulton Educational, London, 1965.

H. J. Schoeps, *An Intelligent Person's Guide to the Religions of Mankind*, Gollancz, London, 1967.

N. Smart, *World Religions: a dialogue*, Penguin, Harmondsworth, 1960.

N. Smart, *The Religious Experience of Mankind*, Collins, Glasgow, 1969.

J. Storer, ' "Hot" and "cold" food beliefs in an Indian community and their significance,' *Journal of Human Nutrition*, vol. 31, pp. 33–40, 1977.

W. A. R. Thomson, *A Dictionary of Medical Ethics and Practice*, Wright, Bristol, 1977.

J. Townson and T. Moorhouse, 'Some basic characteristics of Blackburn's Asian population – 1977', Blackburn and District Community Relations Council, 1977.

J. Townson and T. Moorhouse, 'The socio-economic conditions of Blackburn's largest ethnic minority grouping', Blackburn and District Community Relations Council, 1979.

INDEX

Abortion (*See* Pregnancy termination)
Address forms, 31—32
Alcohol, 13, 16—17, 48, 74, 78
Al-Whudhu, 75—77
Anaesthesia, 42
Anglican Church, 12, 57, 58—67
Anxiety, 16
Autopsy, 79

Baha'i, 47—49
Baha'u'llah, 47
Baptist Church, 63
Bathing, 36
Behaviour, normal and abnormal, 10
Belgium, 24
Beliefs, 1, 9, 10, 11
Bereavement, 17—19
Biological revolution, 4—5
Birth, 19—21
    after, 20
    attitudes to, 20
    before, 19
    during, 19
Blood transfusions, 13, 87, 96, 97
Body, 11, 73, 86, 87
Booth, William, 63
Breasts, 12
Brethren, 14, 65
Buddhism, 8, 49
    schools of, 51—52
Burial, 26, 48, 57, 60, 62, 64, 66, 67, 69, 74,
    79, 84, 87, 90, 93—95, 97—99, 101

Cannabis, 30
Caste, 43
Chador, 22, 45
Change, 4
Cheongsam, 22
Children, 21
Chinese, 20, 31, 33
Christian Scientists, 93—95
Christianity, 53—55, 91
Church (*See* under specific creeds and
    denominations)
Church Army, 59
Church of Christ, Scientist, 93—95
Church of God, 95
Church of England, 58—67
Church of Jesus Christ of Latter Day
    Saints, 91—93
Church of Scotland, 57, 65
Circumcision, 85
Classroom discussion, 103
Classroom teaching, 102, 105

Climate, 21
Clothing, 11, 22, 86, 92
Community relations council, 36
Confidence, 7
Confucianism, 31, 69—70
Congregational Church, 63
Consent to treatment, 22—24, 53, 60, 64, 69,
    74, 84, 90, 93—95
Consultation, 2—3
Contraception, 10, 24, 87, 97
Countess of Huntingdon's Connexion, 63
Courtesy titles, 42
Cremation, 18, 26, 74
Crockery, 86
Cultural aspects, 4, 8, 15—46, 104
Customs, 1, 9
Cutlery, 86

Dangers, 5
Death, 14, 25, 37, 79
Death certificate, 18
Decision-making, 2—3
Developments, 9
Diabetes, 9
Dialects, 8, 38
Diet, 12, 26—29, 43, 73, 84, 86, 93
Dietary restrictions, 7
Doctor, 7
Dried milk, 12, 21
Drinking water, 27
Drugs, 13, 29—30, 48, 74, 78, 79

Eating habits, 28—29
Education, 30
Eightfold path, 51
Elderly persons, 31
Emergencies, training, 103
Emotional difficulties, 103
Emotional factors, 9
Ethical norms, 2
Ethical variations, 2, 5—6, 103, 105
Ethics, 1, 37, 102—7
Etiquette, 31—32
Exclusive Brethren, 65

Face, 32
Family, 2—3, 16, 18, 25, 31, 33—34, 85
Family planning, 24, 48
Fear, 34, 42
Feeding, 20
Festivals, 11, 54—55, 72, 78, 81—83
Folklore, 27, 28, 37
Food, 12, 78
    hot and cold, 28, 74

Foreign languages, 38, 40
Four noble truths, 49
Fox, George, 66
Free Church, 57, 60–67
Friends, 10, 33–34
Funeral directors, 19
Future, 4

Genetic engineering, 5
Genitalia, 12, 45, 46
Gestures, 32
Grief, 17–18
Gynaecological treatment, 45

Hair, 11–12, 73, 89
Handicap, 34–35
Hatha-Yoga, 70
Health care systems, 35–36
Hindu, 20, 26, 43, 70–75
Holy Bible, 11, 20, 56, 59, 64–67, 92
Holy Communion, 12, 59
Holy Water, 68
Hygiene, 36

Illness, 36
Immigration, 8
Indian Mutiny, 4
Indians, 43
Insulin, 9
Irish wake, 26
Islam, 75–80

Jainism, 75
Japan, 33
Jehovah's Witnesses, 13, 95–97
Jesus Christ, 67
Judaism, 80–88
      Liberal, 83–85
      Orthodox, 9, 12, 14, 36, 85–88

Karma, 49
Koran, 11

Language, 8, 37–40
Last offices, 14, 48, 57, 60, 62, 64, 66–69,
      74, 79, 84, 87, 90, 93–95, 97–99,
      101
Legislation, 5
Luther, Martin, 57
Lying in state, 25

Mahayana School, 52
Marijuana, 30
Marriage, 40
Meal times, 27
Meals, 8
Mental illness, 37
Methodist Church, 63
Modesty, 22
Moravian Church, 63
Mormons, 91–93

Mourning, 19
Murder, 4
Muslim, 11, 14, 17, 20, 22, 26, 33, 34, 36, 44,
      45, 75–80

Names, 31–32, 41
Naming, 20
National Health Service, 35
Needs, patient's, 10
Neglect, 3
New procedures, 4
Next of kin, 17
Nirvana, 49
Nursing process, 106

Orthodox Church, 55–57

Pain, 13, 32, 34, 42, 45
Pakistan, 45
Perfluorochemicals, 96
'Playing God', 1
Plymouth Brethren, 14, 65
Politeness, 39
Polygamy, 46
Post-mortem, 18
Poverty, 21
Powdered milk, 12, 21
Pregnancy termination, 48, 64, 66, 79, 93, 94,
      97, 103, 105
Prejudices, 36
Presbyterians, 57
Protestant Church, 57–67
Psychiatric illness, 36
Psychosomatic effects, 6–7
Psychotic illness, 37
Punishment, 10

Quakers, 66

Ramadhan, 78
Rastafarianism, 100
Reading difficulties, 30, 38
Regional accents, 38
Reincarnation, 72
Relationships, 14, 16
Relatives, 10
Religions, 47–101
Religious articles, 11, 47, 52, 56, 59, 62,
      64–66, 68, 73, 75, 84, 85, 88, 92, 94,
      96, 98, 99, 100
Religious factors, 8, 47–101, 104
Religious observances, 11, 47, 52, 56, 59, 62,
      64–66, 68, 73, 75, 84, 85, 88, 92, 94,
      96, 98, 99, 100
Religious Society of Friends, 66
Responsibility, 3
Resuscitation techniques, 103
Rinzai sect, 52
Roman Catholics, 10, 12, 14, 20, 25, 67–69
Russian Orthodox Church, 56

Sabbath, 85
Sacrament of the Sick, 14, 68, 69
Salah, 75, 78
Salvation Army, 63
Salwar-kameez, 22, 45
Sari, 22
Scotland, 57
Sexual intercourse, 46
Sexual matters, 45
Shinto, 90
Shock, 42
Showers, 36
Sickle cell trait, 42
Sikhs, 11, 12, 20, 88–90
Social class, 29, 43–44
Soto Zen sect, 52
Spiritual healing, 93
Spiritualist Assocation of Great Britain,
　　97–98
Sterilization, 24
Stigma, 36
Stress, 7
Subcultures, 15
Superstitions, 37, 44
Symbols, 7

Talmud, 11, 84
Taoism, 91
Teaching, 102–7
　　classroom 102, 105
Terminal care, 13, 48, 57, 60, 62, 64, 66, 67,
　　69, 74, 79, 84, 87, 90, 93–95, 97–99,
　　101
Theravada School, 51, 52

Torah, 11, 84
Tradition, 27
Training, 104
　　emergencies, 103
　　multidisciplinary, 106–7
Transmigration, 72
Travel, 8
Treatment, 13, 16, 22–24, 48, 53, 56, 60, 62,
　　64, 66, 67, 69, 74, 79, 84, 87, 90,
　　93–96, 98, 99, 101
Trust, 10
Two-tier process, 5

Undressing, 11, 22, 45, 73, 78
Unitarians, 98–100
United Reformed Church, 65

Vaginal examination, 46
Values, 9
Vasectomy, 24
Vegans, 73
Vegetarians, 28, 84
Vishnavites, 70–72

Wesley, John, 63
West Indians, 20
Women, 6, 22, 44–46, 73, 78, 89
Writing difficulties, 30, 38

Yoga, 70

Zen Buddhism, 52